the art of downloading music

Printed and bound in Great Britain by MPG Books Ltd, Bodmin

Published by Sanctuary Publishing Limited, Sanctuary House, 45–53 Sinclair Road, London W14 0NS, United Kingdom

www.sanctuarypublishing.com

Third printing, 2005

Cover design: Dan Froude

ISBN: 1-86074-618-7

the art of downloading music

Steve Levine

Sanctuary

Contents

Foreword

Although it is a relatively recent invention, the Internet has woven itself into the fabric of our collective lives. Words like 'email' and 'download' have become a part of our everyday vocabulary and 'attachments' added to emails have given us the ability to send information of all types around the world in seconds.

Nowhere has this technological revolution been more exciting – and more controversial – than in the music industry. Downloading digital music has already become more popular than purchasing singles on CD, and it's not a stretch to say that it's the format of choice for a new generation of music listeners.

The Art of Downloading Music

MP3 players in general, and the iPod in particular, with its massive storage capacity and ease of use, have tranformed the way many people listen to and purchase music. Never before have you been able to carry around most, if not all, of your music collection in your pocket. Combined with iTunes, the iPod represents an entirely new way of maintaining and adding to your music collections.

Yet, like most things, the digital music revolution also has a dark side: illegal downloading, which deprives artists, songwriters, and producers of their income, has been the scourge of major record labels that were slow to realise its significance. The record companies are now catching up, with an increasing number of 'official' download sites popping up, assuring downloaders of high-quality versions of their favourite songs – and royalties at last being distributed to the rightful copyright owners.

Having been a successful record producer for over 25 years, the ability to download and send audio files over the Internet has revolutionised the way I do my work. I can, for instance, start a backing track in London, have guitar parts added by a colleague in California and then send the finished mix to anyone in the world with access to a computer.

And therein also lies the problem.

With all this technology at our fingertips, the learning curve can be quite steep for those not already familiar with the ways of computing. Facing what they see as a truly daunting task, many quit before they even get started.

Hence the need for this book.

The Art of Downloading Music leaves out all the techno-speak and cuts to the chase, helping you get up and running and downloading as fast as possible. It answers many of the most commonly asked questions (and in my career I've been asked many) and shows you the neat tips and tricks that you can pick up along the way. It's a book I wish I'd had years ago; you'll be enjoying the digital music experience in no time.

Happy downloading,

Steve Levine

Introduction:
The Future Is Here

'It is not the strongest of the species that survive, nor the most intelligent, but the one most responsive to change.'

Charles Darwin

It could be said that music, more than any other traditional form of art, is something that is meant to be shared. Part of what makes a live concert such an electrifying and unforgettable experience is the element of communality, a unifying event that you can discuss afterwards with friends and peers as you lord over ticket stubs, t-shirts, and memories for years to come. Music is both an intensely personal, yet ultimately universal experience, and nothing speaks so clearly to teenagers as do their favourite artists. It's hard to imagine a painter or novelist entertaining thousands of screaming fans, while for most popular musicians, such treatment is de rigeur.

And it is teenagers who are the most computer literate, adept at adopting new technologies with relative ease. (It is said that most teenagers spend upwards of seven hours a week online, and much of that is devoted to finding and downloading music.) Perhaps this is why new technologies like peer-to-peer file-sharing programs have been adopted so effortlessly by the music-consuming public, of which teenagers comprise a significant percentage, and whose tastes in music, albeit loyal to a fault, are fluid and impressionable all the while. But over the past quarter decade, since the first home personal computer was introduced to the market, sweeping changes in technology have revolutionised the musical landscape as we know it. The advent of the Internet, the 'open sourcing' of software and technologies like that used by Napster, the cultural imperative to 'keep up with the Joneses,' have all contributed to how music is produced, purchased, consumed and experienced. What would Bauhaus and the Cure be without a serious Goth fanbase, or the Sex Pistols and the Ramones without the punks? From performer to producer, from band to DJ, music has always been a communal experience – something to be shared with family, with peers, with anyone who has a love of music.

But the definition of 'share' has changed dramatically over the years. From the early dubbing of tape cassettes to current legal file-sharing services such as Apple iTunes and the new incarnation of Napster – as well as illegal ones like Kazaa and Morpheus – vast changes, prompted by technological developments, have brought what was once a behemoth of an industry nearly to its knees. Somewhat ironically, over the past six years, almost at the same time as music labels were undergoing massive mergers to form five powerful corporations, individuals were developing the technology to subvert a system the labels were doing everything in their power to maintain. In 1999, one such individual, the 18-year-old college dropout Shawn Fanning, AKA 'Napster' (a nickname earned by a shock of 'nappy' hair that he tamed with the aid of a baseball cap), created a code that allowed users to share compressed music files, AKA MP3s, via a centralised file server, with anyone else in the world equipped with no more than a computer, modem and a copy of his program. Little did he know it would be a shot heard (literally) around the world.

History has taught us that the prohibition of any mutually beneficial exchange is doomed to fail. Take a woman named Carrie Nation, and one of the least successful campaigns in history – the Prohibition. Her life (as she perceived it) marred by alcoholics, she took a hatchet to her local saloons in Kansas where alcohol was, at least on the books, illegal, attacking individual establishments in order to spread her message and contempt for the widespread flouting of the law.

Fast-forward a century, and replace Carrie Nation with the Recording Industry Association of America (the RIAA), and the Prohibition with the current downloading 'crisis', and you might gain some insight into the current situation. Much as Carrie went for individual saloons, the RIAA is going after individual file swappers in an attempt to combat illegal file-sharing on a case-by-case basis. But such methods have proved to be extremely unpopular, the media portraying the RIAA as a ham-fisted Goliath who is stomping out Davids with tiny bedroom 'operations' in order to maximise their profits. One *New York Daily News* cover story detailed the plight of a 12-year-old

Catholic school student named Brianna LaHara, who faced a potential multi-million dollar lawsuit for downloading sitcom soundtracks and nursery jingles like 'If You're Happy and You Know It'. It was eventually settled for far less ($2,000 and her mother's promise that LaHara would never illegally share files again), but it was, for the most part, a serious public-relations blunder for the RIAA. However, the association remains convinced that the lawsuits are serving as an effecting deterrent against piracy, and as of May 2004, 2454 individual lawsuits had been delivered.

Recent studies have shown that while popular file-swapping services like Kazaa have decreased quite radically in popularity since the RIAA initiated the lawsuits (according to a recent *PC World* article, Kazaa currently has 20 million users, down from 35 million less than a year ago) many other smaller peer-to-peer services are flourishing under the radar. And research indicates that the number of people using peer-to-peer services has remained more or less stable over the past nine months - a pretty safe bet that downloading music from the web isn't going out of fashion any time soon.

So, what are the record labels and artists whom they represent to do? The writing was on the wall, and it said if they weren't ready to make serious changes in the way they managed their business, they were going to go under. Why would fans buy music from stores if it were available at the touch of a button, and for free? The past five years have shown that the downloading of music is not simply a fad – it's too easy to learn, too convenient to dismiss, too ubiquitous to ignore. In a climate where millions of people now shop for everything from prescription medicines to used cars online, it seems highly unlikely that random lawsuits will stop illegal file-sharing any more than the threat of an IRS crackdown will one day eliminate tax fraud.

To put it simply: If you can't beat 'em, join 'em.

Last year in the US, amid some scepticism, Apple introduced the first legal option for those jonesing for a legal download fix – the iTunes music library, available for download for free or packaged with OS X on a Mac. By reaching an agreement with the Big Five and hundreds of indie labels, Apple secured the rights to sell the music online – individuals tracks for 99 cents, and entire albums for $9.99, with the labels, artists and Apple, all receiving a cut of the profits. In June 2004, a version of iTunes for the UK, Germany and France was launched, with plans for a Europe-wide version by the end of the year. Others (like

MusicMatch, Rhapsody, Sony Connect, even Walmart) have followed in its wake, though none of these have a music library or a custom media player like iTunes. Virgin Entertainment Group will also be joining the fray with its Virgin Digital entertainment platform, and will launch its independent download store later this year. In addition to downloads, Virgin's music store will offer music management software and subscription services, and will be backed by the online Radio Free Virgin Internet radio stations which will be linked to the Virgin Digital service. But Apple, which bundles hardware, software and a portable player – the iPod – into a tidy, easy-to-manage package, is by far the most successful of these ventures, reaching 70 million downloads within its first year of inception and over 85 million to date. 'Digital music is going to eventually supplant hard goods, and any retailer who is ignoring that fact is doing so at their own peril,' Virgin Digital president Zack Zalon was quoted in a recent issue of *Billboard*. It seems the labels have finally caught on.

One thing that has slowed down the universal adoption of iTunes and other downloading services has been a lack of cooperation by some marquee artists. Artists like Madonna and Led Zeppelin remain in digital purgatory, while other big-name acts have exclusive deals with competing services, where fans can go to buy music, album art, tickets and more. The Beatles catalogue, however, which has been unavailable as a legal download until now, may soon be available – sources say that representatives for the group have been in talks with several online music providers. Insiders speculate that when the world's most popular rock group's entire catalogue is available for download could well prove to be the watershed moment in digital music history.

Another sign that the tide is turning are artists that are gearing their album-release campaigns with digital downloads in mind. The Beastie Boys, for example, released their entire catalogue online on 27 April, a day before premiering their brand new single, 'Ch-Check It Out,' exclusively on iTunes. The complete new album, *To The 5 Boroughs*, was released on 15 June, and is now available on iTunes.

Even more startling is the fact that the stony-faced RIAA will, come August, include digital online sales (from legitimate sources) when determining a song's eligibility for gold and platinum status. Sales of 100,000 singles will earn a gold award, with double that amount required for a platinum award. CDs must achieve higher figures to receive

RIAA awards, with gold at shipments of 500,000 copies and platinum at 1 million units. In the UK, the first ever download singles chart will be debuted in September 2004.

And the future looks even brighter for those who like their music wherever they are, whenever they want it: mobile phone retailer T-Mobile recently launched a service that allows customers to download music to their mobile phones. In the UK, where there are perhaps 50 million GSM mobiles, this could have major impact in terms of market share – Forrester Research estimates a $100 billion global market in four years' time.

As more people discover how easy it is to download music, these numbers are sure to increase dramatically. It would be optimistic to say that all of these downloads will be legal, but with programs like iTunes making it possible to preview a clip of the music before downloading it, browsing, purchasing, and enjoying music is becoming easier than ever before. And with the record labels and the RIAA tailoring their business to meet the needs of a tech-savvy generation, digital downloads would seem to be the wave of the future. In fact, it's almost impossible to imagine a future without them.

A Conversation with Steve Levine

Let's start with the basics. What exactly is an MP3?
It was invented by a group of German scientists in 1987 as a way of shrinking video files down to a manageable size to run on computers. They did it by stripping away as much data as possible from the sound and the visual files – all the stuff that listeners and viewers theoretically don't notice. After the code was approved by the International Standards Organisation, it became known as ISO-MPEG Audio Layer-3, or MP3 for short. Then it hung around, waiting for a handful of maverick music fans and computer geeks to see its real potential.

A Conversation with Steve Levine

How did it become the main way that people swap music files on the Internet?

Music fans began using it to encode and swap bootlegs of things like Grateful Dead concerts. A few sites sprang up using MP3s to showcase unsigned new music acts and even to sell downloads by established names. But then a 17-year-old lad from Massachusetts called Shawn Fanning wrote a very clever piece of code that enabled people to connect to the web and share all the music stored on their computers with anyone else in the world who wanted to copy it. He sent it to a small group of computer hacker friends who improved and refined it, then in June 1999 made it available through a site called napster.com. Napster became big so quickly that the music industry didn't even realise what was happening until it was too late.

The industry eventually took legal action – as did the hard rock band Metallica, who were furious that people could take their music without paying for it. Napster has been forced to change, and it now offers legal music downloads for PC users. But by then it was too late – the idea was out there, the computer program that enabled it was refined and rewritten by countless others, and now there are thousands of sites where music fans can illegally share their music collections with other computers around the world.

The Art of Downloading Music

Why the MP3?

Because it was a readily available format that seemed to translate very easily and it squashed the data rate down to almost nothing. On a CD an album comes to 650MB for an hour's worth of music. So even with broadband, if you want to transfer a full-quality album in one go, you'll have plenty of time to go and put the coffee on! An MP3 reduces the file size down quite dramatically with some loss of the original quality. How much quality you lose depends on the song. Certain songs squash down well and the MP3 sounds pretty good. Other songs really do sound terrible. But what's brilliant is, you can squash it down small enough that you can effectively attach an MP3 file to an email. And suddenly storing your entire music collection on your computer becomes practical.

It won't be CD quality, of course. But then we all also know that you can have an awful-sounding CD or fantastic-sounding CD depending on how it was made. The same applies with an MP3, but even more so. You can have a badly encoded MP3, which will sound really terrible, or you can have a brilliantly encoded MP3, which will be very representative of the format. And even within MP3 of course, there's the different bit-rate that you use to encode, ranging from fairly bad right up to quite good. But as you move from quite good to very good, the file size is doubled each time. The best-quality MP3 file is four or five times the size of the lowest-quality file that you can encode. So it's always a trade-off. I prefer to carry less music around on my iPod, and to have a better quality sound.

If I'm sending an artist a song, just so they can hear the performance, I send it by email. I can squash it right down and that's fine. I can even send it in mono to halve the size yet again. If they want to listen to a mix in their car or at home, the sound is far more important. Then I'll give them an MP3 at the highest rate that I can. I can send them, say, a 320kbps stereo file that will take about two minutes to download. It would still be better if they took a CD with them, but sometimes it's easier to send it via the computer.

Are there any alternatives?
The MP3 wasn't designed initially as a compression tool specifically for music. It's been adapted and it's worked incredibly well, but now people are realising that it could be improved. Apple has its AAC encoding – which is, theoretically, better sounding – and there are some new MP4 versions coming out. Formats for compressing music will continue to improve. Hard drives are getting bigger and better. And as more of us get access to faster broadband

connections, the need to compress the files down to quite shockingly low sizes may disappear. But I think a certain amount of compression is always going to be needed, otherwise you'd need a terabyte of storage space on your MP3 player to get 10,000 songs on. That's impractical.

When did you first become aware of music online?
Pretty much as soon as I was on the Internet. I can't even imagine a time without it now. I lived in California from 1990-93, and I remember visiting a musician friend and him showing me what the web had to offer, and there's that first moment when you go, 'Oh my God, Pandora has come out of the box!' I started using email fully around 1993, when I did some consultancy for a company in Palo Alto, California. They were right on the cutting edge of technology and they were using emails to attach updates to the software they were asking us to test. Even though I wasn't thinking of music initially, I realised straight away that this kind of file transfer was just fantastic. To be able to get a software update immediately and not worry about discs and everything was great. And then music followed.

And how did you get involved with music technology?
I always loved music, but I was never really interested in being in a band. I wanted to be the person who made the

records. At first, I thought that was the recording engineer. Later, I came to realise that the person with the real creative input is the record producer, but that was after I started working at CBS Studios in London. This was 1975 and there were no engineering courses at colleges as there are now, so I just went to studios on days off from school and asked for a job. I came in at a time when the technology was changing very fast, and because I was still learning and wasn't set in my ways, I found it easier to pick up than some of the more established engineers there.

As my career progressed and I became a producer, I stayed at the cutting edge of technology. In 1984 I bought a Fairlight, which was the first device to offer digital sampling and playback on a keyboard. It cost £55,000, and gave me the ability to record small samples of sounds, store them, manipulate them and play them back on a keyboard. It's an unfair comparison in some ways because there were barely any personal computers around then, so the Fairlight was a powerful machine, custom-made to create music, but now with the right software and a keyboard you can do similar things on a fairly cheap laptop. When I produced bands like Culture Club in the '80s, I worked in big studios that cost thousands of pounds a day. Now I can record to the same quality in a small home studio.

The Art of Downloading Music

As the technology moved on, I moved with it, adding to my knowledge bit by bit. Now I find I'm often working with younger artists who are, frankly, daunted by the technology. They may be coming to you with some fantastic ideas but they don't know how to realize those ideas and a lot of the time is spent chatting and trying to glean from them what they want, then using my skills to get that for them.

It's funny to think how things have changed. When I was at school, we did experiments with the computers. This involved sending away punch cards to Nuffield Science Labs and then waiting a week for the results. My first computer had a few kilobytes of RAM in it and now I'm screaming because I want more than 8 gigabytes of RAM! In the last decade especially, the progress has been astounding. It's as if we'd moved from the Wright brothers' first flight to the latest state-of-the-art Eurofighter planes in ten years.

And now you can carry up to 10,000 songs – an entire library of vinyl albums – around with you on a little pocket-sized device.

I used to travel with a bag full of MiniDiscs, and still you'd end up searching through them and realising you haven't got the one track you really wanted to hear right then. Now I can take it all on one tiny iPod – that's so liberating. Though not all MP3s are the same, and if you encode your CDs at the highest quality as I do, you're not going to fit 10,000 songs. Nor are you going to get near CD quality yet. But you've got to put it into perspective. Do I want to take a trunk of CDs around with me on holiday, or do I compromise on quality to be able to enjoy a wide choice of music while I'm sunbathing?

Were you a big Napster user?
I've never used Napster. I could never get it to work properly on my Mac. And I didn't need to, because I have such a vast CD collection that I've usually got what I want anyway. Before the iTunes store was launched in Europe, if I did need to find some obscure thing, I'd use Limewire.

But as soon as I saw it, I thought file-sharing was dangerous for the music industry, particularly as they were ignoring it, rather than embracing it. That concerned me. I've always believed you should keep your friends close and keep your enemies closer, and they didn't do that. Instead the record companies thought, 'Why would they want this? It's such horrible quality compared to our beautiful CDs.'

They'd just made a ton of money in the 1980s when everyone switched from vinyl to CD, so they assumed that people would always want better quality. An MP3 is worse than a cassette tape when it comes to sound quality. You've got the hiss on a cassette, but on the whole it records much better quality than an MP3. And when you listen to an MP3 of a song and then listen to the CD version, of course you're going to prefer the CD.

But people also want their music immediately, and that's what downloading offers. The big record labels failed to understand the impact of it. Before too long it was like the Wild West out there on the Web, and it has taken them far too long to catch up.

Is there any way back now that we've become used to taking music for free?
People have nothing against paying for something if they perceive a value. Look at the way concerts have taken off. We're happy to pay substantial sums for tickets if we can see that we're going to get a great evening's entertainment. The trouble was that by the mid-90s, the main record companies were looking like big conglomerate ogres. There were a whole series of mergers and take-overs and the main companies got bigger and bigger, until they

were seen as huge corporations that cared little about their artists. There was also a series of high-profile court cases in which major artists like George Michael and Prince were suing their record companies, cases which made the record companies look like ogres.

People who are file-sharing think they're ripping off the record company, not the artist. And they don't care about stealing from a big conglomerate, which is not the right attitude, but the record companies brought that on themselves to a certain extent. The problem is that the label may be earning the lion's share of the royalties, but when you steal a track, the poor artist's smaller percentage gets lost as well. With a lot of the classic tracks, those artists are on appalling deals anyway. And when you download for free, you're stopping them getting even those tiny royalties. We need to educate people about that.

But why should I pay for music if I can get it free?
First, I put food on the table for my family as a result of receiving royalties from my record sales, and I still deserve those. But also the huge success of the Apple iTunes store in America – it sold more than 75 million downloads in its first year, 2003 – proves that people are happy to pay for guaranteed quality. The files being sold by legal sites like

iTunes are encoded from the original recordings, the master tapes. They're the best quality available. When you download from the free sites, you never know what you're getting – often it's a very poor copy of a copy of a copy. On illegal sites like Kazaa, people may have downloaded MP3s, burned to CD, then re-imported that CD and re-encoded it again. So there's no guarantee of the quality.

Also of course, there's the convenience. Not only do you know what you're getting, but you can do it quickly and easily. How many times have you messed about looking for a track and either been unable to find it, or the download has cut off halfway through?

What the record companies need to do now is to offer that same sort of service and give value. With bands that are really into their fans and their music, when you buy the CD, you get extra stuff. You can have extra tracks to download, access to special areas of the website, copies of the videos on the disc – whatever you want. And people will buy the CD if they can see that it's worth the money and they're getting more from it.

There will always be people who steal, and there will always be bootleg CDs that have been mass-manufactured by pirates, but that needs to be stamped on because it's wrong and it's killing the industry.

Yet you're excited by downloading?
I think it's fantastic, it's a whole new frontier. It can only be positive, but it just needs to be welcomed with open arms. If you hear something you like on the radio, download it from sites such as the iTunes store .You can have a copy of your own to play in minutes, all for 79p. That's fantastic. When my kids hear something they like on the radio, they want it immediately. They don't want to wait, and they don't necessarily want to buy the whole album.

They recently heard Maroon 5 on the radio, for example. They loved the first single and downloaded it. That made me buy the album for them, which they absolutely loved. Then they logged onto the band's website, which is great, with loads of things to interact with. And if you join the fan club on the site, you get first pick of the tickets for their live shows. So the moment the new tour dates were announced, they automatically sent my daughter an email telling her. We bought tickets through the website, they arrived in the post, and she's really looking forward to going. Now that's a band doing a great job at maintaining contact with their fans, and that's how it should be. She hasn't spoken to the band, she's had no direct contact with them, but she's got a connection with them.

So in the short-term, I think we'll have more retailers like Napster and Connect selling downloads in ways similar to the iTunes store. Then we'll have individual bands offering the same service of their music through their websites.

Where will that leave the big record companies?
For me, the only role really left for them in the long-term will be maintaining their back catalogue, making sure they look after the masters and reissue the best ones. They'll continue to sign new bands, but they'll be bands that have already been tested in the marketplace. They're no good at developing acts any more. A new band will need to make their music, release it, tour, build their fan base and if it's all working, the record companies will come in to move them to the next level. But in the meantime, the band will have sold 5,000 units via their website or whatever.

The good thing about the iTunes store is they've said they will take independent music that they feel is good enough. If iTunes and other sites like it really become a shop-front for new talent, it can only be healthy. Then the artists will be getting the lion's share of their money, the record companies will be getting the smaller share, and the situation will be reversed.

But the public have also got to realise that as with everything in our lives, big corporations exist. They're not going to go away. You can clip their wings occasionally to make sure they behave, but you'll never get rid of them. Beating up record companies won't hurt them, but it hurts their artists really badly. I don't think people appreciate how devastating it is for an artist to have his royalties taken away. The kind of people who are downloading music for free wouldn't take a trolley into a supermarket, fill it up with food and then walk out with it without paying. It's the same principle, isn't it?

Ideally we'll get a situation where a lot of these sites do what Napster has been forced to do and go legitimate, so a royalty can be paid when people download from them. The thing with the worldwide web now is there is no time frame and there is no distance anymore. So you've got to make everything available to everybody at all times, legally. Then the law can concentrate on chasing those who are doing the real damage.

That's not a kid in some bedroom somewhere with 20 tracks on his computer that he's downloaded for free. It's not right, but it's not killing music in the same way as these villains who have factories manufacturing fake CDs, making up sleeves and passing them off as real. That is what's killing it, because the public is buying something that they think is a legitimate product and they're being conned.

A lot of people download music without realising that that's what they are doing – they just see it as getting a new ring-tone for their phone.
Again, it shows that people are willing to pay for a service they enjoy – they're happy to pay £3 for a ring-tone. It's weird actually, because you spend all this time making records and then the ring-tone can sell more than the record!

But it's still quite a lot of work to make a ring tone. You're so restricted. You're restricted to a number of notes, and the polyphony of some of the phones is different. You're having to compromise to fit in with the technology, so it's odd producing them. Although in the next generation of phones, the sound is improving. On the next lot you can supply the sounds. So, as a record producer, what you could do is to work with the band, take stuff off the original master and use that as part of the ring-tone, if you wanted to go that mad.

Let's go back a bit. Did you buy the Diamond Rio or any of the early portable MP3 players?
I've always looked for new ways of carrying music around with me. I was one of the first producers to buy a 24-track digital tape machine for my studio, which was manufactured by Sony. As a result they let me buy one of the first portable CD players ever – it had a separate battery pack, which itself was the same size as the player! Then I went to MiniDiscs. I wasn't tempted by the early MP3 players because they looked like they were going to be a novelty. They didn't have enough storage to make them worthwhile. But the moment the iPod came out, I thought, 'That's definitely it!'

By then I was already using the iTunes software to store my music library on my computer, because it was such an easy way to access your music. Once you've gone through the hassle of physically putting your CD into the drawer and encoding it, all you have to do is type in the artist's name or part of the title, and it comes up immediately, ready to play. I don't have to spend ages searching through my CDs to find a certain track.

The Art of Downloading Music

Why is the iPod so good?

It has an iconic design. That's why it was so successful initially. Essentially, it's just a hard drive with fairly unsophisticated software and a little LCD screen, but it's so simple and easy to use. The scroll wheel seems obvious now, with the way the whole front of it looks like a speaker box, but of course it wasn't obvious at all when Jonathan Ive and his team were designing it – they thought about levels and sliders and all sorts of other things. When something is designed so well, you almost forget that it was ever designed at all. It's the same with a great song – it becomes so much a part of your life that you can't imagine a time when that song didn't exist.

The manufacturing quality on the iPod is superb. It's interesting that they've managed to get a level of finish that is normally only ever achieved by the Japanese. There's such an eye for detail too – each one has its serial number laser-etched on the back, instead of a nasty-looking sticker. You can also have it personally engraved as my daughters have done, which is a fantastic service because then it makes it much more of a cherished item. Even the white headphones helped make it immediately different. And once you've imported your CDs into iTunes or downloaded your music from the net, it is a phenomenally easy thing to use. It's very intuitive, and it is a fantastic product.

I love the fact that there's nothing you can touch; you can't take the back off it easily and fiddle with it. The MiniDisc is open and you can see everything that's going on, which is dangerous. You can see that it looks really fragile and if you don't put that MiniDisc in properly, it will bend everything. And of course the discs themselves can break too. The iPod has this invisibility, as though there's nothing going on, even though it's probably whirring its heart out inside.

It's the same as when the Walkman first came out, it had an iconic shape and it was a touchy-feely product. In 50 years' time we will look back on it as being the device that moved everything forward. The iPod wasn't the first portable file player, but it was the one that changed the market forever.

The 'shuffle' button on the iPod has changed the way many of us listen to music. Letting it play through your music at random throws up all kinds of interesting combinations, or suddenly it'll play a great track you'd forgotten you even had.

The Art of Downloading Music

It's great when you get certain playlist combinations that you wouldn't naturally do. On train journeys particularly, I find that quite exhilarating. Sometimes I have to grab a pen and paper and write it down, because it's thrown up such a good combination of songs. And it's so easy to put a whole CD in, whereas if you were making a compilation for a MiniDisc or whatever, you'd only put in your favourite tracks because space is limited.

On your iPod suddenly you'll hear a track you hadn't listened to properly and realise it's brilliant. I was given a brand new album of a new band recently, and I heard it and instantly really liked one of the tracks. But I quickly put the whole lot on my iPod, and I've now discovered two other tracks on it that I think are fantastic, and which maybe I wouldn't have listened to. Because the iPod has such a huge capacity, you cast your net wider and if you play it on random it does throw up some incredible surprises.

My iPod sits next to my computer in the studio, and I use it as my archive source. When I'm talking to an artist and they want to hear a particular track, I can just play it instantly without having to run upstairs and find the CD. One of the tracks we're recording at the moment is the result of finding a rare track that I had in my collection, but I'd overlooked. I put in the wrong word and it came up. I gave it a listen and thought, 'Oh my God, that's absolutely perfect!'

Is there anything to compete with the iPod?
Not at the moment for me. The iPod has set the benchmark and although there are other players with interesting features, right now they all tend to look like imitation iPods. Perhaps someone will find a different way of doing the same thing – a different interface, or maybe more advanced software that does certain things better. We'll always want even more songs, and more capacity to enable us to encode music at higher quality. Maybe there's a format that's yet to be discovered. Future players could store vast quantities of data, compress it to keep the size down, but play it back at good quality.

As people got educated with CDs, they realised that not all CDs sound the same and they began to appreciate those that sound better because they're better recorded, better engineered. Then you start buying better machines, because although you can go to Argos and buy a CD player for a few pounds, it's not going to be as good as a beautifully engineered player from a company like Denon.

It'll be the same with the iPod or whatever portable file player eventually replaces it – as the market matures, people will want higher quality. Right now none of them are delivering even close to CD quality. I work very hard on the records I make, and it's a bit depressing to know that the MP3 may be the possible first choice of listening. It's almost back to the '60s, when studio engineers would mix something that sounded great in the studio, but most people would hear it as a vinyl record playing scratchily on a Dansette player.

Some major record labels have tried to stop us playing CDs we've bought and paid for on our computers. Do you agree with this?
As a producer of copyrighted material, I don't want my material being copied on everybody's machine. I'm happy for them to enjoy it, but there has to be a trade-off between your right to enjoy the music I produced and my right to get paid in some way. The same applies to an artist and songwriter.

I think you have to restrict people's ability to copy it indefinitely, forever and ever. But perhaps the better way to do it is to offer some sort of key. If I want to use some of my software, it could come with a dongle [a digital key]. If the key is not in the machine, I can't use it or download free updates. If it is, I can – on any machine I choose.

With music, this would also have to come with some kind of phenomenal service that only registered users can have: offer tickets ahead of release dates, offer special bonus stuff or pre-release material. Record companies need to be involved and to involve their audience. It's not that hard.

Acts like REM already offer free downloads to fans via their websites. Can you envisage a future where major acts – people at the Madonna, U2 and Eminem level – don't sign to record labels and simply sell their music online?
Definitely. Look at what Simply Red have done. When they came to the end of their deal with Warners, they decided not to renew it or sign to another label. Mick Hucknall had a big fan base, and he knew who those fans were, so he decided to do it himself. He set up his own organisation, SimplyRed.com – the name not only of the label, but also the website. He'd made enough money to be able to pay for the new album himself. He recorded it in his home studio, manufactured it and then licensed it through various outlets – and of course he also made it available via SimplyRed.com. He's sold about a million

units so far, which is less than he sold with his old label, but he's now making 90 per cent of the money, not 10 per cent.

It was a big risk, especially considering how much he's spent on the TV advertising. None of this comes cheap; he's had to have big balls and deep pockets, because that's what you're paying major record companies for. Basically they're acting as a high-interest bank – no one else would lend you the money for such a high-risk venture. Simply Red had their own bank balance and they've done it themselves. And there are bigger acts than Simply Red. The most important thing is: how do you attract people to your website? That's very important.

Marillion did it a different way when they found themselves without a record deal. They wrote to their fans and asked them to pay in advance for an exclusive copy of the new album, thereby giving them the cash flow to make the record. The fans loved that. More and more successful bands could do it themselves. It is a new technology and as the technology matures, it will become easier. But it's harder for the new bands because they need to break and they need the infrastructure.

What do you think will happen to record shops in this brave new world?

If they adapt, nothing at all. People still like to touch and browse and shop. Maybe shops will have download stations. They'll definitely have to offer all sorts of other things, and they'll have to work to make the shopping experience really pleasant. And there will always be room for specialist shops with really informed staff.

When computers first came out with word processors, people said soon you'll never have to buy a book again. We're now buying more books than ever. Music is the same. We'll use it differently, but most of us will still want the physical product — whether that's a CD or something else. Maybe there'll be a new way of presenting it. A lot of CDs have started to come in DVD-sized cases with more booklets and things attached. Maybe the CD will become only part of the package you'll buy. There is room to do new and exciting, innovative stuff. You've got to keep changing.

How do you use downloading in your work as a record producer?

Obviously, the Macintosh is the hub of my hard-disk recording system, so I have a powerful machine to do all that. All the tracks I work on are composed, written, and produced on computer.

Artists often want to listen to examples of things, either to hear specific sounds or the general feel of a track, or because they're looking for songs to cover. I use my iPod to search out and play stuff that I already have, or I'll go online to search for something that I don't have, or just to check if there's anything else out there. Sometimes I'll find another version of a song that I wasn't even aware of, and I'll listen to the arrangement just to see if there's a different view on it. So that's one use.

Then I use high-quality full-bandwidth downloading for other members of the act or other musicians who are working on a track with me. With the track I'm working on at the moment, for instance, my friend Hank in Los Angeles will be doing the guitars. When we've finished the backing track, I'll send him an MP3 attached to an email just so he can hear where we're at. In parallel to that I will upload full-quality files onto my server. He will then download those and be able to open the same song on his computer in Los Angeles. We will then phone each other – or possibly use our iChat to talk – and we'll discuss what overdubs he's going to do. He's got a similar studio to me in his home, so he will record the guitar parts while I'm asleep tonight. He will upload them onto the server when he goes to bed, and when I wake up in the morning I'll download them and put them onto my computer. That works brilliantly. There's no creative need for us to be in the same place or to be working at the same time.

Then when I've finished the mix, I'll email it to the artist as an MP3. Again, an MP3 doesn't show everything on a mix but you can get an overall feel for it. I would prefer them to hear the CD on a proper sound system, but it's very, very handy to be able to send it to them quickly just to check things. Or perhaps they want to check a vocal performance, and say If they don't like a line of it. There we're not listening to quality, we're just listening to performance, and MP3 is fine for that. It's fantastic.

You have teenage daughters. How are they using this technology?
In the same way that I am. And more so! My two are incredibly computer-literate. They've both got iPods; they are downloading feverishly and encoding feverishly. The thing is they can't imagine a world without it. They laugh at my old vinyl records.

The Art of Downloading Music

There's something I'll never forget. When my oldest daughter was three or four, she had one of those singalong cassette tapes. One day she was trying to put it into the video machine saying, 'I've heard them sing it, now I want to see them!' It was real kid's logic: why shouldn't you have a medium that does everything? And now we're getting to that stage for real.

Part One - Getting Started

FAQ on Downloading

When it comes to facts, there is no shortage of conflicting opinions. Nowadays, what passes for wisdom in local bars or at cheap resorts usually amounts to almost anything you want to hear. The important things that most people leave out are context and credibility – two things which are too often in short supply. Despite a plethora of friendly facades, the Internet is still a prankster's paradise and not everything you might see or hear necessarily matches reality. But that doesn't mean it can't be fun – particularly now that you happen to be the proud owner of a trendy new iPod. Often a new experience can create new dilemmas and when it comes to downloading music, the uninitiated frequently have a lot of questions – like what the FAQ does this chapter heading really mean?

Without getting into an over-heated philosophical discussion on the digital degradation of language, let's just say that once you get online, you may get the feeling that everyone out there is speaking another language. Whether you choose to blame it on the cursed intrusion of business-speak and text-messaging or just generally on a failed education system, you will, to some extent, have to get your head around a variety of acronyms and linguistic bullets that attempt to 'simplify' concepts and information that would otherwise require a thoughtful and reasoned explanation. Explanations for most of these conundrums can be found in areas called FAQ, which is online speak for Frequently Asked Questions. For example, now that you've got your iPod, you will at least have a passing familiarity with something called MP3. But the question is, do you actually know what an MP3 is? Do you know why – or even if – you'll be using it? Are you aware there that are other alternative digital music formats like WAV, WMA, RA and MIDI as well?

OK, so before we run through all those other 'frequently asked questions' you've been formulating, why don't we take a quick look at the options you have when choosing a music format.

> **hint**
>
> Music isn't just big business. When it comes to space, it's just plain big. Music, at least in the format that it's stored in on a CD, is just too fat to put online. Just one minute of music needs around 10MB of disk space. This means that the average four-minute track takes around three hours to download with a bog-standard 56K modem. Even if you've got broadband you're still looking at around half an hour. If you start to consider DVDs, which can hold up to 12Gb, you could be looking at months or even years to download anything significant – assuming your hard drive could handle it.

Digital Music Formats
MP3

MP3 files have the extension '.mp3' and are available for download from many web sites and stores. MP3 (MPEG-1 Audio Layer-3) technology compresses a sound sequence into a very small file which is usually one twelfth of the original file size. Obviously, this is a good thing when you're downloading music from the Internet. The designers of the

MP3 compression algorithm managed to do this by eliminating sounds that the human ear cannot perceive. While MP3 technology is particularly impressive, it has been abused by music pirates since one can very easily create MP3 files from commercial CDs and make them available for downloading. That's why the RIAA, major music companies and most governments have been cracking down on the distribution and sharing of MP3 files in this manner.

WMA

WMA or Windows Media Audio, is Microsoft's proprietary music file format that Uncle Bill is, as one might expect, currently marketing aggressively. WMA files are smaller in size than MP3 files, but still retain a decent level of sound quality. This format is gaining popularity on websites for sampling music and also in certain other portable music players. However, whether WMA will overtake the popularity of MP3 remains to be seen.

WAV

A wave file is characterised by the file extension '.wav' and provides raw, uncompressed audio data. Originally invented by Microsoft, wave files are still used widely, such as in the start up and shut down sounds for Windows. Its audio quality isn't bad, but the file size is huge. A full song title in wave format may take up to 30MB of disk space or more.

AIFF
The AIFF or Audio Interchange File Format is a popular music file format used in the Macintosh operating system. In a way, you could say that they are the Macintosh equivalent of wave files, although it may not be exactly true. AIFF files have the file extension '.aif' when accessed via a PC and they contain raw audio data which result in excellent sound quality but also take up a large amount of disk space.

MIDI
The MIDI, or Musical Instrument Digital Interface file format, was originally created for recording and playing music on digital synthesisers. MIDI files are very small in size because the MIDI file only contains information on how music is produced (eg note-ons and note-offs). It relies on whatever sound card you might have to play back the MIDI file information and play back the music you've created using an inbuilt sound card wavetable.

RA
RA or RealAudio files support streaming technology and

were created by Progressive Networks. RA files are highly optimised for live, streaming audio from websites and are best played back on RealAudio players which are freely downloadable from Progressive Networks.

> **tip** As you might expect, there are many software applications which can convert music from one format to another (eg MP3 to WAV or WAV to AIFF). Try doing a search for these applications at www.macupdate.com.

OK, so now you know that the MP3 format is a compression system for music and that it helps to reduce the number of bytes in a song without noticeably hurting the sound quality. Essentially, the goal of the MP3 format is to compress a CD-quality song by a factor of 10 to 14, without losing the CD quality of the sound. So, for example, a 32 MB song on a CD compresses down to 3 MB or so on. MP3 and lets you download a song in minutes rather than hours, and store hundreds of songs on your computer's hard disk without taking up that much space. But then again, maybe that just raises a few more questions. So, here are a few more FAQs for your consideration.

Is the sound quality of MP3 better than a CD?

No. Because MP3 is a compression format, it throws away some of the information from a CD format and uses characteristics of the human ear to design the compression algorithm. For example: There are certain sounds that the human ear cannot hear, so the MP3 does not include them. There are also certain sounds that the human ear hears much better than others, so if there are two sounds playing simultaneously, an MP3 format will only include the louder one.

By cleverly using such facts about the human ear, certain parts of a song can be eliminated without significantly damaging the quality of the song for the listener. Compressing the rest of the song using well-known compression techniques shrinks the song considerably, roughly by a factor of 10 at least. So, when you've finished creating an MP3 file, what you have is 'near-CD' quality. No, the MP3 version of the song will not sound exactly the same as the original CD, because some of the song has been removed. But it will be very close indeed.

Where can I find MP3 files for my MP3 player?

All you need to do is type 'MP3' into any search engine and you will find that there are literally thousands of sites on the

Web where you can download MP3 files. Or, save yourself some time and go directly to the iTunes Shop.

> **tip**
> To convert your CD songs into MP3 format, you will need:
> - a computer
> - a CD-ROM, DVD-ROM, CD-R, or CD-RW drive (internal or external)
> - ripper/encoder software

Can I record music from CDs for my MP3 Player?
Yes, if you have a CD collection and would like to convert songs into MP3 files, you can use ripper and encoder software to convert them. Although 'ripper' was also the nickname of Giles in *Buffy the Vampire Slayer*, in this context it merely copies the song's file from the CD onto your hard disk. The encoder compresses the song into MP3 format and by encoding songs, you can play them on your computer or take them with you on your iPod. Ripper and encoder software usually comes with MP3 players.

Specific instructions will vary with individual software programs, but we'll look at how you can do all this with your iPod a bit later in the book.

Can I record music from my MP3 player to a CD?

Yes, if you have a writable CD drive in your computer, you can convert (decode) your MP3 files into full-size CD tracks and then save them onto an audio CD. This allows you to listen to your favourite MP3 files on any normal CD player. WinAmp also has a plug-in that will create full-size WAV files from an MP3 file and some encoders will also decode. Once you have the full-size CD tracks, the software that comes with your CD-R drive will let you create an audio CD easily.

Is MP3 legal?

The short answer of course is yes, MP3 is merely a data compression format. However, what you do with that format can be legal or illegal. The distribution of music in MP3 format over the Internet has prompted much legal debate and action over copyright law. (See the 'War on the Web' section of this book.) In fact, the Recording Industry Association of America won a suit against the original Napster over illegal distributions of MP3 files. Although Napster is now back online as a legal pay-for-music service, this issue will become increasingly important as new music data compression algorithms become more readily available. A good site for news about developments in Internet music is ZDNet Digital Audio.

Apart from the occasional out-of-copyright recordings of obscure Sumerian singalong tunes, street-legal download-quality music available online will fall into roughly two categories:

1 Free Previews – authorised by the artist, publisher or record company
2 Pay Sites – which operate on either a song-by-song basis or via some sort of subscription service

Songs that you find on legal download sites are:

- In the public domain
- Uploaded by artists who are trying to get exposure
- Released by record companies trying to build interest in a CD
- Paid for by you for the right to download, and the site pays the artist and/or record company royalties.

What is sampling rate?

Sampling rate is how often samples are taken from the original music signal. The higher the sampling rate, the better the sound quality. However, the higher the sampling rate, the greater the storage space needed for the file.

How many songs are available on iTunes?
At the rollout, there were 200,000 songs in the library, although this is far from a historically complete collection. Apple adds songs quite regularly but some albums are still only partially available (ie they have tracks missing). Although Apple has secured exclusive rights to a few dozen songs by artists such as Bob Dylan, U2, Live, Sheryl Crow, Coldplay, and several others, there are glaring omissions such as the Beatles and the Rolling Stones' entire catalogues. On the other hand, there are 51 Elvis Presley albums available in whole or part, and the iTunes Shop is the first place that the Eagles songs have been available for download. The opening page of the Music Store changes constantly, and new selections are added all the time

How much does it cost?
Individual songs are 99 cents in the US, 79p in the UK, most albums are $9.99/£7.99, or less if they have fewer than 11 tracks. Naturally, there are exceptions to the rule.

Oh yeah...like what?
Some albums are not sold on a song-by-song basis. Others

are only sold by the song, so you end up paying, for instance, £11.88 for a 12-track album. Others have one 'anchor' song that cannot be bought except as part of an entire album.

If there are other companies already offering digital music downloads, what's so great about Apple's store?

Leaving aside the aforementioned legal issues, the 'competition' essentially breaks down into two categories: the subscription-based services and the peer-to-peer networks. iTunes Shop is completely different to either of these. As mentioned above, some subscription services charge a flat monthly rate for varying levels of service, but you end up only 'renting' the songs. As soon as you cancel your subscription, any music you have downloaded runs the risk of becoming unplayable. Peer-to-peer networks such as Napster and its progeny, essentially offer file-swapping software that usually acts in wanton disregard for intellectual property rights and copyrights. However, in exchange for letting anyone rummage through your computer's hard drive, you get the opportunity to do the same to theirs. While there are loads of ways of demonising this sort of system, the worst bit is that you're never really sure what you're going to get in terms of sound quality. You also run the risk of importing a malignant and malicious code into your system that could otherwise be stopped by a firewall.

Right, so now that I know about sound formats, are these songs in MP3 format?
Er...well, no. Apple has chosen Advanced Audio Coding (AAC) as the format for all the songs on iTunes. (See why you need FAQ?) AAC is part of the MPEG4 standard and was developed by Dolby Labs who owns the licensing rights. In addition to being marginally better than MP3 at a given file size/data rate, it also allows much better control over who is authorised to use a given song. The marginally better quality, according to Apple, means that every song can be encoded at 128kbps, roughly 1MB for every minute of music and an 11-fold savings in file size from the original, uncompressed audio file. 128kbps is the most-often cited file size for MP3 files intended for play on portable devices, as it is 'good enough' for most people's ears in the relatively noisy environment of an aeroplane, a commuter train, a car, or with non-audiophile headphones. Apple claims that since AAC is superior to MP3 at the same bit rate, 128kbps equates to CD-quality for most ears on most consumer-level equipment.

So how do I go about making a purchase?
Credit card details, address, and other pertinent information is stored in your Apple ID, and with a single click you can buy and download any of the 200,000+ songs. If you prefer, iTunes gives you the option in the preferences panel to employ a 'Shopping Cart' where clicking on a song or album simply adds it to a queue of songs ready for purchase. When ready, clicking on the 'Buy Now' button at the bottom of the Shopping Cart page will initiate the download of all purchased songs and charging of your credit card.

Maybe I'm being thick here, but does that mean if I buy 15 songs in "1-Click" mode, I will see 15 charges on my credit card for 99 cents or 79p?
No, if you choose to remain in 'one-at-a-time' purchase mode, and buy 15 songs over less than a 24-hour period, all 15 are aggregated into a single transaction on your credit card statement.

What are the system requirements, beyond Mac OS X?
Until recently, the requirement was a credit card with a US address, Mac OS X 10.2.5 or later, a connection to the Internet (broadband recommended), 256MB RAM (recommended), and iTunes4 or later available as a free download from Apple's website. Quicktime 6.2 (also a free

download) is required to fully exploit the AAC capabilities of iTunes4. Apple has made the iTunes Shop available to Microsoft Windows and has recently opened the service to the rest of North America and the world – or at least more of the world.

What about the extras that come with 'real' CDs, like liner notes?

Sorry, for the moment, all you buy for your money is the digital file(s) containing the music as well as a medium-resolution image of the album cover. Unlike a regular CD, you need to supply the physical media upon which the music is stored, be it a CD-R, hard drive, or inside a portable music device such as the iPod. If you've really got your heart set on liner notes, you should factor that into your decision whether to purchase from the iTunes Shop or not.

Given the pressures on record shops these days and occasional sale offers, why should I use iTunes?

Well, let's see...you can shop 24/7 from the comfort of your arm chair. You still pay a lot less for just the songs you like off an album, and you get the album art with single-song purchases. You get immediate gratification because your purchase is downloaded right after you click to make the purchase and you don't have to drive home from the mall.

And perhaps best of all, although it is still dependent on the record companies digging their master tapes out of their vaults, there is a much higher possibility of seeing rare, out-of-print albums for sale on the iTunes Shop than in the shops because of the cost commitment to press thousands of physical CDs.

OK, let's say I don't have a Mac. What are the requirements for iTunes with Windows?
You'll need a PC with a FireWire port or Windows-certified FireWire card, or a PC with USB2.0 port or a Windows-certified USB2.0 card along with Windows ME, Windows 2000, or Windows XP Home or Professional.

If I have iTunes for Windows installed, how will AudibleManager work with iTunes?
You can use AudibleManager for downloading Audible content from www.audible.com. You'll then need to add the Audible content into iTunes so you can play, transfer to your iPod, or burn an Audio CD.

Do I need to install iTunes for Windows to transfer to my iPod?
Yep. AudibleManager can transfer Audible content into your iPod, but only if the iPod services software is installed.

Why can't I use AudibleManager to connect to my iPod now that I have installed iTunes for Windows?

We're talking Microsoft here, remember? Installing iTunes for Windows disables 3rd party software like AudibleManager from connecting and transferring to the iPod. So, you're expected you to use iTunes for transferring content to your iPod.

Why do I have to use a 2-step process and AudibleManager to download Audible content and then add into iTunes?

Providing support for Audible Content in iTunes for Windows has been a major undertaking for both companies, and for the initial launch, the 2-step download and then add process is required. Audible and Apple are working together to provide a more seamless process in the future.

Right, so how do I add my Audible files into iTunes for Windows?

First you need to find where you download Audible content. By default, they are found in the C:\Program Files\Audible\ Programs\Downloads directory. If you have changed the default location for downloads, in AudibleManager go to Tools - Location of Download Files, and it will tell you where the downloads are. Then in iTunes, go to File \ Add to Library and select the Audible download folder.

What formats can I transfer using iTunes for Windows to the iPod?
You can download and transfer formats 2, 3 and 4.

Both AudibleManager and iTunes allow CD Burning of Audible content. Which one should I use?
Use the software that you feel most comfortable using. AudibleManager has a couple extra features and will place track marks every 7 minutes on the CD for easy FF/REW navigation. You can also print out CD labels with the AudibleManager software. Use iTunes you to create a playlist and then start burning the Audio CD.

OK, then. It's about time we got online!

Getting Online

'The future exists first in imagination, then in will, then in reality.'

Barbara Marx Hubbard

Online services like iTunes let you download a huge selection of songs and then play them back on your computer, burn them onto a CD, or simply listen to them at your leisure on a portable player like the iPod. So, just how difficult is it to 'get online'? Well, unless you've been living in outer Mongolia for the past few years, you're probably already aware of the fact that it's not all that difficult. For that matter, even if you have been living in outer Mongolia for the past few years, you probably know roughly how to get online anyway.

As any advert for the various computer outlets will tell you, technology is becoming progressively more intuitive and easy to use. However, as with most things, the theory is always slightly more attractive than the practice and even with a properly user-friendly system like the Macintosh, a lot of Internet providers aren't quite as friendly and accessible as the digital mythology would have us believe.

Your Modem: Your Friend

Nowadays, you can access the Internet through all sorts of gadgets like PDAs, mobile phones and occasionally, the good old television. However, to really get the full-on Internet experience, you still really need a PC or Mac equipped with an appropriate network device called a modem. Although modems used to be separate add-ons, these days nearly all new personal computers come with a standard dial-up modem built in and ready to connect to your phone line. However, dial-up services have hit a speed ceiling and if you're serious about downloading music, video or other media services, than you might find them a bit slow. Because there are so many different

Internet subscription offers these days where you pay a flat fee per month, this isn't always a major consideration for many home users. But if you do feel the need for speed, in most areas now you can get some sort of broadband connection. This generally costs a bit more and also requires a different kind of modem, usually supplied by your chosen broadband provider. Once you have all the relevant equipment, you'll also need an Internet account with one of the many Internet Service Providers (ISPs). Most of these offer increasingly competitive packages.

It's the ISP that essentially acts as a gateway between your computer and the rest of the Internet and you can choose from a wide range of dial-up access or other faster systems such as ISDN, ADSL or in some regions, cable. All give you full access to the Internet, just at varying speeds and prices. When you get your Internet account, you'll also get at least one email address thrown in. Occasionally, you might even get some free web space to post your own site. Some providers offer a half dozen or so email addresses but be aware that if you decide to change providers at any time, you'll lose these addresses with the account. There are a number of free services such as Hotmail which are easy to get and don't tie you to a particular ISP. However, such services aren't exactly the same as email. Instead, they're something called webmail accounts which do allow you to send and receive messages from your own computer or from Internet cafes, libraries, etc if you don't happen to own a PC or Mac yourself. While Hotmail is quite popular, it's worth checking out the myriad of other similar services which often work a lot better.

Broadband is faster than normal dial-up modems because it offers a higher bandwidth, which is simply a term used to describe Internet connection capacity. Bandwidth, usually described in bits per second (bps), provides a measure of the speed at which you can download music, video, etc from the Net. The standard dial-up modems that come with most PCs and Macs are only capable of providing a relatively low-bandwidth connection – usually at around 56000bps or 56K. Cable, satellite and ADSL usually fall within the broadband category because they can move more bits. The other important point about broadband is that it's an 'always on' Internet connection and you can generally still use your phone while you're online as well.

Online security
When it comes to downloading music, or any other

Internet service, the question that always arises is, 'How safe is it to use my credit card online?' Well, in most cases, your credit card details are safer online than when you pass your card to someone in a bar or restaurant. Although there have been occasions where individual's credit card details have been stolen and misused, most reputable Internet sales sites are extremely secure. Just make sure you read any advice or instructions thoroughly before making any online transactions.

These days, even if you don't actually own a PC or Mac, there's bound to be somewhere near where you live or where you work where you can rent time online. There are loads of reasons why being online outweighs any effort or hassle you may endure in learning how to usa a PC or Mac. And, best of all, once you're actually online, there's a whole world-wide community of other people just like you out on the Net where you can find an endless variety of hints, tips and individual help with practically any problem that may possible arise. And once you're hooked, you'll probably find yourself helping others as well.

Equipment You'll Need

Practically any new computer, whether it's a Mac or PC, will be more than powerful enough to get you online. As a bit of personal advice, don't get completely sucked in by what we like to call 'processor envy'. In other words, you don't really have to buy the most powerful and trendy machine available at the time. Sure, there are advantages in having the top of the range system – if you can afford it. If you're an average home user and you simply want to surf the Net and send emails, you can get by with any of the many economical bundles on offer. However, if your main ambition is to create and handle sophisticated graphics, video or music production, or you plan to indulge in a lot of heavy usage downloading music, videos, etc, there's no denying that the more powerful your system, the more comfortable your actual user experience will be.

Probably the biggest decision you'll have to make, if you're starting from scratch, is whether to opt for a Windows PC or an Apple Macintosh. Like the Harley Davidson, the Macintosh has a style and image that, though much imitated, can never be truly copied. All of the aspects of 'user-friendly' computing that we take so much for granted today, including the graphic desktop, icons, the mouse and WYSIWYG (what you see is what you get) graphics and text, was first brought to the mass market and popularised by Apple.

For those of you too young to remember the bad old days, the first IBM PC came with a horrible and annoyingly complex operating system called DOS – marketed, though not actually developed, by Microsoft. PCs quickly became synonymous with Microsoft. Eventually, Microsoft was dragged kicking and screaming into the 20th century and responded to a growing demand for an easier user interface with the development of Windows – initially a poor Imitation of the Macintosh interface stuck onto the original DOS core. Microsoft PCs have traditionally dominated, and still dominate, the corporate business world. Macs, on the

tip The iPod is actually a clever hard-drive. It's so clever, Apple can sell a single iPod model that works for both Macs and PCs. Although Mac and Windows PCs use different formats for their hard-drives – Macs use a file system called HFS Plus while Windows use something called FAT32 – the current iPods all come pre-formatted for the Mac. However, once you run the CD installer software that's included with the iPod, if it detects that you're connected to a PC, it automatically re-formats the iPod with the FAT32 system. You don't even have to think about it...

other hand, have traditionally been and continue to be favoured by the more creative industries and individuals working in areas such as design, publishing, film and video and music production.

Despite all the scare tactics about compatibility and the amount of software available, you can essentially do almost anything online with either a Mac or a PC. It's all down to personal preference. A lot of people say that Macs are always more expensive than PCs. However, because a Mac has an operating system that includes sophisticated sound, graphics and design features, you'll probably find that to configure a comparable PC system, with add-ons that actually work, you'll end up spending pretty much the same.

hint

You can use the USB2 cable for any iPod from 2003 or later, including the new iPod Mini, with your Windows PC. However, if you've got a Mac with USB2 jacks, you can only connect the iPod Mini. Normal full-size iPods require a FireWire connection.

System requirements

Since your iPod is designed to communicate with your Mac or PC, it's worth knowing that for music downloads, at least, your system requirements aren't particularly onerous. Essentially, all you need is:

* Enough Horsepower

If your going for the Mac option, you'll need at least 256Mb of RAM and at least a 400MHz G3 processor. If you want to go the PC route then you're looking at at least a 330MHz Pentium (or equivalent) processor with at least 96Mb of RAM. If you happen to be running Windows XP, make sure you've got at least 256Mb of RAM. Remember – when it comes to memory – bigger is better.

* A Reasonably Recent Operating System

While it's probably best to use the latest version of OS X on your Mac, especially if you've got iTunes4 or later, you can use System 9.2.2 if you've got iTunes2. On a Windows PC you'll need to be running either Windows 2000 or XP unless you're using the MusicMatch Jukebox software. In which case, you'll need Windows ME, 2000, or XP.

* The Right Connections

To make the right connections you'll need either a FireWire or USB2 connector. Most Macs after 1998 have FireWire built in but you'll find that FireWire jacks are only now beginning to appear with any frequency on Windows PCs. If your PC doesn't have FireWire, it might be possible to add a FireWire card or use USB 2, which is actually faster than the original FireWire. As it happens, USB2 has become a standard feature on new Macs and PCs and it is possible to install it on older machines using a range of USB2 expansion cards.

The philosophical and existential arguments surrounding the Mac vs PC debate could fill a book in its own right – or at the least a geeky doctoral dissertation. In most cases, Orr's law always applies – 'Whatever the thinker thinks, the prover will prove.' The best advice when it comes to choosing equipment, is simply to think about what you want to use the computer for, think about what you may want to use it for in the future, consider the size of your bank balance and then decide accordingly. Do shop around and don't jump at the first attractive deal you encounter. Nowadays, apart from specialised software and certain games, much of the software available runs equally well on both the Mac and PC. Even boring business stalwarts like Microsoft Office look and run the same on a PC or Mac and file-sharing is completely seamless. If you're buying new, even when it comes to the iPod, both Mac and PC users can use the same software to manage and organise their musical content. The free program from Apple, iTunes4.5, looks and works identically the same in its Mac and Windows version. However, if you're a PC user and don't happen to have Windows 2000 or XP, the bad news is, you can't use iTunes. But don't panic. As indicated earlier, software like the MusicMatch Jukebox will allow you to manage and move music to the iPod, copy songs from CDs to your PC and perform most of the other functions available with the iPod.

So far this year, 500,000 songs have been bought online in the UK. In the USA, iTunes has sold 85 million tracks since it was launched just over a year ago. And online services aim to sell 12 million downloads in Britain next year, which is roughly equivalent to a quarter of all singles sales at the moment. On top of that, world-wide sales of CDs were down by 7 percent last year and so far, in 2004, British sales have fallen by 4.3 percent in value. But while downloading music online represents possibly the biggest revolution in the music industry since the advent of the CD, as a phenomenon, it is still sending chills down the back of the record industry. There's still a lot of other interesting stuff out on the Net that you might like to explore once you've got online. And the best thing about the online world is that there's always something new.

What's New on the Web

The Internet has often been compared to the Wild West of 19th century America. Everyone is rushing for gold, but essentially, it's still a wild and lawless place full of con men, gamblers, outlaws and an assortment of down-home honest folk trying to offer interesting goods and services to an incredibly diverse global audience. Like the implications of the old Arlo Guthrie song, 'Alice's Restaurant', you literally can get anything you want – and in some cases, that might even mean Alice.

Want to watch some bizarre Japanese short films? Help solve an episodic mystery or check out some cutting edge animated cartoons? No? How about watching a music animation video or perhaps you'd rather have your tarot cards read? Or how about singing along, Karaoke-style, with Looney Tunes characters or dabbling in a bit of Chaos Magick? Still not interested? Well, there's always all those self-indulgent writer's sites, places to buy fetish furniture, or the ones where you can play real-time games with people all over the world, or help write things like interactive screenplays. In other words, welcome to the diverse and discordian world of amusement and entertainment, Internet-style, a business that aims to reach all the parts that no other traditional business could even hope to reach – all in one handy global consensual hallucination.

There's a bit of something for everyone on the Web and only one thing is certain: it's all in a state of flux. Sites are constantly being revamped, more video and audio is being made available for downloading and new 'networks' and special interest areas are starting up all the time. In the area of entertainment, there are three major sub-categories:

- original content

- promotion and marketing by major entertainment corporations

- news and information about show business, celebrities and other stuff

Of these three, by far the largest is the third. You can find out just about anything about anything somewhere on the Internet. The major trick, however, is learning how to discriminate between real information and 'disinformation'. Because there's no official editorial control on the Internet, much of the information out there can often turn out to be either opinion (informed or otherwise) or a hallucinatory collection of words. As a source of news and views, the Internet does, however, often scoop the rest of the broadcast media.

Information comes in a variety of forms and flavours and currently there's more material about show business and the music industry than you could possibly imagine, including reviews of movies and television shows, gossip about actors and actresses, databases about old movies and long-dead entertainers, clips of new movies and interviews with celebrities and musicians. Sometimes the information is only text-based, but more often than not, it comes with still pictures, audio or video clips or animation. Money also is being poured into an increasing number of promotion and marketing sites. However, for many of us, probably the most interesting area is original content.

In the first few years of the Web's existence, several highly touted original entertainment and games sites created a stir, drawing thousands of users to their sites and leading to a brief spurt of Internet-based productions. However, the upshot of many of these early failures was that most major Hollywood producers backed away from creating new entertainment for the Internet and instead adopted a watch-and-wait stance. However, they did – and do – continue to use the World Wide Web as an electronic billboard for established brand names as well as for exclusive previews and promotions.

In most cases, that boils down to promoting and marketing new movies, television shows, home videos and record albums. There isn't a media company in the country that doesn't have a presence on the Web and some are going to great lengths to lure online users to their sites. Time Warner and Disney, in particular, have reportedly spent hundreds of millions of dollars to build up their online presences, creating offshoots of their movie, television and publications empires. The reason? According to Warner Bros Online, it's because the people who buy their music, watch their shows and buy tickets to their movies are streaming onto the Internet.

The emphasis currently remains on promotion and information, particularly since the advent of broadband, satellite and other high-speed Internet access services. Available content now includes of plethora of programming like news, talk shows and comedies, but there are also channels dedicated to women's issues, hip-hop music, skateboarding, the occult, anarchy, science fiction and more. One of the biggest selling points for the Internet is that much of the programming consists of content that can't be found anywhere else.

An increasing number of innovative sites vaguely resemble the old variety show concept. They feature everything from cartoons, music and fiction to games and commentary. Much of it fresh, often irreverent or offbeat. Some of it is just self-indulgent. However, there is a range of sites that showcase the work of fledgling artists, while others show off other creative and commercial capabilities. Sites built to feature Flash technology designs combine all the latest bells and whistles with original programming – including some adult-humour animation – and appears to depend heavily on fresh content. Another innovative and entertaining place to visit is the Shockwave site (www.shockwave.com), featuring animation and games that showcase the Macromedia's newest technologies.

Some of the best-known entertainment sites on the Web are those created for movies. Such sites have been obligatory ever since the first one appeared in 1994 for the movie *Stargate*. Hollywood folklore has it that the web site for *Stargate* created such a pre-release buzz that it played a pivotal role in bringing moviegoers out on opening weekend. Today, most feature films have Web sites that, at the very least, outline characters and present a variety of video clips. Others, such as the sites for *The Day After Tomorrow* and *SpiderMan2*, are elaborate and often designed with serious input from the producers and directors.

Television networks and cable companies also have a full presence on the Web, again primarily to promote their programming. And Guild writers are slowly being drawn into the area as well. More and more video-related sites are developing as well and downloading films, TV programmes and DVDs will become increasingly popular as more and more users get high-speed connections.

Original entertainment in the form of music, movies, and games on the Internet is still evolving, but it's definitely not an area anyone can afford to overlook for sources of tunes, movies, photographs, games or merchandise. While you may be spending most of your time downloading music to your iPod, it's worth taking the occasional stroll in cyberspace and sampling the myriad of goods and services available in other areas as well.

Part Two - Brass Tacks

What Are Downloads?

According to an ancient Arab magical text, to hear music whenever you want it, you need to evoke the name of a djinn called El-Adrel. You don't need a lot of complicated hardware for this, but in order to get in touch, you also need to wear a metal cap on your head or he won't come. Once you've got hold of him, or have made the connection, he will speak to you from a pot of water that you will already have placed on a table near you. To avoid any hassle, make sure you speak to him fairly and he will then enable you to hear whatever music you wish. When you want the music to cease, simply call his name the other way round, and he'll go away... and take the music with him. The only problem is, you must not call him more than once each day, so make sure you've given some thought to your selected playlist. However, if you're not a full-fledged discordian prankster or a committed chaos magician, you might find downloading music from Internet sites such as iTunes a little easier.

Any operation which essentially copies a file, image or song from one computer to another is called a file transfer. When that file is heading for your machine from somewhere else, eg, the iTunes Store, that file is called a download. In most cases, a download of any sort simply copies the selected file to your hard drive and leaves the original undisturbed at the source. If you, on the other hand, send a file from you machine to a web site or another computer, it's called an upload. Since an upload can change or delete other files, you normally need some sort of permission from the server or file destination before you can upload anything significant.

Apart from music, the Internet is a virtual warehouse of freely available software, images, music, videos, etc. OK, so a lot of it isn't what we might call genuinely free and some of it is probably downright illegal. But there's still a lot of it out there and what you choose to do with it is entirely up to you. Although you can download stuff from other people's PCs or Macs, these days, most of the downloads anyone is interested in come from the Internet. And the Internet is definitely becoming the place to look for the best selection of music – new and old.

For those of you who only download the occasional file or program, your favourite browser, although not always the best tool, should be more than adequate. Both Explorer and Netscape are, theoretically, supposed to be able to resume downloads if your connection unexpectedly drops or your computer crashes. However, in practice, this doesn't always work. And, unless you're using a Mac, Explorer can't even show you a list of all the downloads currently in progress. Which means, occasionally, you could get 90 per cent of a file downloaded and then have to start all over again because your phone line dropped or your computer crashed. That's why PC users favour separate download managers which can reduce the risk of errors, speed the whole process up a bit, show you all your current downloads and even show-off by searching for alternative mirror locations while telling you which one is the quickest.

File size and modem speed determine just how long a download will take and you'll find that all files available for downloading are usually compressed to decrease their transfer time and to reduce storage space. Earlier, in the

FAQ section of this book, we looked at the various sound file formats that you will encounter when downloading music. More general file compression formats that you may encounter include WinZip, UltimateZip and Stuffit Expander on the PC and the Mac. You can also expand these files, for example, expanding a Mac file for PC use, by setting the appropriate options under Cross Platform or Download Options.

Apart from the obvious benefits, such as the ability to obtain music while in the comfort of your own home, downloading is also an essential element in important activities such as keeping your operating system and browser up-to-date. While new versions of these are always loaded with new features, the primary imperative for updating you system and browser is simply to get all the bugs fixed. The same applies to getting hold of the latest drivers for your extra devices such as printers, modems and video cards, and it's also the most convenient way to get hold of various plug-ins for media players such as QuickTime, Shockwave, RealPlayer and Windows Media Player.

Once you've downloaded a good number of music files onto your Mac or PC, you don't have to leave them on your hard drive. The MP3 generation has spawned a plethora of Walkman-like portable players which can hold thousands of songs and are, well...portable. Although we obviously think the iPod is the best of the bunch, if you are still shopping around for an MP3 player for your music downloads, there are a few things to look out for when you're shopping around:

- What's the connection and does your system support it? As mentioned earlier in the book, these pocket jukeboxes may sport USB, USB2, or FireWire connectors for uploads. If you buy a player with one of these, and your computer doesn't have one of the same, you're flat out of luck. It simply won't work.

- How much memory does it have? Since you need to allow for about 1MB per minute of music, don't go for anything too small. Even if it's expandable, compare cost with other models before buying. As a point of reference, the iPod currently holds more music than any other MP3 player available.

- What's the battery life? Buying new batteries all the time is a bummer. The iPod provides a built-in rechargeable lithium polymer battery that will give you up to ten hours of continuous music on a three hour charge.

- Is it upgradeable? (And if it is, how much will it cost?) If you can't download software upgrades, the whole thing could become obsolete before you've had time to throw the packaging away.
- How small is it and how much does it weigh? Remember, these are portable devices supposedly designed to be carried around and used in a variety of activities and environments. Don't let yourself be embarrassed by an overweight music player.

- How good is the display and can you read the track titles?

Once you've got your music downloads onto your hard drive, you can also burn your music onto a CD or DVD, depending on the model of Mac or PC you happen to own. In most cases, you will have to convert MP3s or things like Windows Media Files to the WAV format before you can burn them onto a CD. Fortunately, a lot of modern CD burning programmes now do this sort of thing automatically once you specify that you're creating an audio CD. Burning your songs to CD is very cheap these days, even compared to the cost back in the old days when people made cassette tapes of vinyl albums. Just make sure you buy writeable CDs that are designed to handle music. You'll be able to fit between 74 and 80 minutes of music on a high quality CD-R disc. As an alternative to downloads, if you want to import music onto your hard drive from a CD, you'll have to convert the music to a digital sound file with a program such as iTunes. In the trade, this is called 'ripping' a CD. Ripping an entire CD is quick and easy and you will also get all the track information such as the artist's name and the album title.

Using sophisticated tools such as the iPod and iTunes, anyone can easily create a personalised digital jukebox that can be played back at the click of a button anytime, anywhere. Despite the paranoia still perpetrated by many record companies, developments like downloads and iTunes will inevitably change your music buying and playing habits for the better. And whether they like it or not, that's what really matters.

War on the Web: the Law of Downloading

These are dark days for the suits of the music business. What other industry could take quite such a gratuitous kicking from consumers and still be accused of complaining and profiteering? How many solvent companies do you know with customers who'd rather steal than buy? And where else are hard-headed entrepreneurs reduced to jelly by technology?

In truth the record business hasn't yet caught the bus to oblivion. Yet chilling figures churned out by the International Federation of the Phonographic Industry suggest that executives need to check the timetable. The next decade will decide whether they stay or go.

In 1996 worldwide music publishing was a $40 billion sector. Seven years later it had crashed 25 per cent to $32 billion. The biggest-selling album in the US – Linkin Park's *Hybrid Theory* – sold just 4.8 million copies in 2003, that's fewer than any best-seller since 1966. Oh for the days of Michael Jackson's *Thriller* (26 million), Pink Floyd's *The Wall* (23 million) or Zep's *Led Zeppelin IV* (22 million).

How has this happened in a world of sophisticated marketing techniques and a ubiquitous mass-media? Simple. *Hybrid Theory* was illegally downloaded for free 4.3 million times from just one Internet file-sharing service. There are plenty of others out there in the ether. The IFPI reckons that more than 2.6 billion music files are pirated every month, roughly 53,000 per second. The number of blank CDs bought to copy music off the net is around 2.2 billion – roughly the same as the number sold legally in shops. Roll up for the Great World Wide Information Highway Robbery.

So how have the bad guys got away with it? Firstly, they don't see themselves as bad guys. 'People who are adults now are aware that they're doing something wrong in stealing other people's work,' says Jim Stoddart, chief executive of web security company Harrier. 'But this taboo is breaking down. When this generation have children they're not going to teach them that breaking copyright is wrong.' Secondly there's a perceived wisdom that record-companies are rip-off merchants charging way over the odds for cheap CDs. There's certainly some truth in this but does anyone seriously believe that because a can of Coke costs, say, 5p to make and 60p to buy, it's OK to steal Coke? Music, it seems, is not regarded as a 'proper' commodity.

Finally, and crucially, there are clear risks involved in shoplifting CDs from record stores. Online – at least until now – it's been soooooo easy. All you need is a PC, internet access and a tiny, free, downloadable application that recognises MP3 music files. Log onto one of the free file-sharing sites such as Kazaa, Gnutella, Morpheus or the original Napster (more of this later), tap in the track you want, sit back and pour a beer. Your computer will check to see if any other registered user has a copy. If two users have it, download time is halved. If 10,000 have it…well, you get the picture.

The track will eventually be copied to millions of PCs, burned onto blank CDs and compressed for use on portable MP3 players. In truth, illegal downloading has never been easier, especially as today's teenage music-lovers are also tech-heads. They've grown up with computers and are unfazed by cutting-edge software. In fact, the global music piracy business was founded by a 19-year-old college dropout – Shawn Fanning – who in 1999 launched Napster.

From the record companies' point of view the nightmare has hardly begun. It has taken around 30 years for PC sales to go from 0 to 1 billion; by 2008 analysts say the total will pass 2 billion. This explosion will be fuelled by a vast, untapped market in China, eastern Europe, India and Latin America and by the growth of broadband (the Internet telecommunications system which drastically reduces file download times). All these users will surely love the notion of free music. They will also benefit from better quality MP3 files and the portable music revolution currently being led, of course, by the iPod.

With its capacity for storing up to 10,000 songs in perfect digital quality, iPod is the techie toy of the moment. It is a de rigueur fashion accessory for celebrities and, according to one Yahoo survey, a fifth of young British backpackers said they wouldn't leave home without one. The iPod is the best-selling MP3 player on the market achieving sales of 700,000 in Britain within a year of its launch in 2002. Together with the online record shop iTunes, it is Apple's Big Idea for the future.

In the first quarter of 2003, music sales accounted for just $25 million of the company's total $1.48 billion revenue. In May that year iTunes launched and sold one million MP3 downloads at 99 cents a track inside the first week. If this trend continues Apple chief executive Steve Jobs will retain his god-like status among his shareholders. But, as he knows, you can move from triumph to tragedy very quickly in Computerland.

Which seems an appropriate moment to briefly recount the troubled history of Apple and its feted Macintosh computer. There's something about a fanatical Mac-user which rather frightens the horses; perhaps because he or she is more cult-follower than customer. That said, the Mac operating system remains the only serious challenger to Windows and is widely regarded as superior. But for one strategic error Apple, not Microsoft, would now be King of the PCs.

Jobs and his partner Steve Wozniak began work on a prototype PC in 1975. They built the first one in Jobs' garage the following year and promptly founded Apple Computers with a third man, Ron Wayne. Four years later they floated the company on Wall Street and the stock increased by 1700 per cent in its first year. By the time the Macintosh was unveiled on 24 January 1984 the business looked unstoppable. Its technology was so advanced that the Pentagon banned all exports to Russia.

Then Apple went pear-shaped. The following year Wozniak left and a bitter feud began between Jobs and his Chief Executive Officer John Sculley. This ended with Jobs quitting and the long road to meltdown in 1997 when Apple's sales collapsed amid debts of $1 billion. The reasons for this are endlessly complicated (don't ever ask a Mac-lover his view unless you have a sleeping bag with you) but most people accept that whereas Microsoft sold Windows licences cheaply and widely, Apple jealously guarded its own crown jewels. No surprise then that hardware giants like IBM chose Windows as their operating system.

Jobs returned to Apple in 1997 and immediately sought a closer relationship with Microsoft. This brought accusations of a sell-out from the Mac faithful but the accounts told a different story. Within two years Apple had annual profits of

$601 million and was selling – in Jobs words – 'one Mac every six seconds'.

If the future now lies with iTunes, iPods and online music then both Apple and the record companies must fight the net pirates. Like all wars, this one has two key components; the dirty business of killing (requiring corporate lawyers) and the battle for hearts and minds (requiring big-name stars). There's even a touch of psychological warfare in the shape of spoof MP3 files, unleashed by the studios in an attempt to 'strangle' pirate servers.

The lawyers killed off Shawn Fanning's original Napster site with consummate ease. Essentially, Napster argued that it didn't infringe copyright because it didn't steal or hold music files; it was just a means for others to swap them. This sophistry cut little ice with the courts and in 2002 the bankrupt company filed for liquidation. Two years later the brand name was re-launched in Britain – this time selling online music legally.

Not all pirates are so easy to sink. Napster had a central server and a US presence but other file-sharers such as Kazaa are de`centralised and effectively use home PCs as mini-servers. Ownership tends to be split among an intricate web of companies, making it difficult to decide who gets the writ. Besides, Kazaa is refusing to die nicely and is alleging anticompetitive behaviour by the music business. For its part the Recording Industry Association of America had sued almost 2000 illegal downloaders by the start of 2004 – including a 12-year-old girl and a 66-year-old grandmother.

The long-term answer is to persuade the public that copyright is ownership; that a song belongs to somebody. This can be an incredibly dull area of commercial law but the nuts and bolts of it is brutally simple and has been enshrined in international legislation for at least two centuries. Artists have the right to earn a living from their creativity – often a royalty payment – and so they should decide how and where their work is reproduced; be it on paper, vinyl, CD or the internet. The theory is that this protects commercial backers and gives talented people the financial security to produce great art. Copyright is distinctly different from plagiarism, which centres on the theft of an idea (such as a similar-sounding melody) rather than reproduction of a clearly defined work.

Leading stars are now being wheeled out by the industry to ram the message home. 'I am excited about the opportunities presented by the Internet because it allows artists to communicate directly with fans,' says Elton John in his endorsement of the war on piracy. 'But the bottom line must always be respect and compensation for creative work.'

Praga Khan, of Lords of Acid, is more forthright: 'It is turning into a catastrophe, especially for artists in our genre of music,' he says. 'We make techno music - so the guys are always playing with their computers. Our target audience are therefore 'techno-nerds' who download huge amounts. I can tell you that we have definitely lost 40 per cent of our sales.'

There's even a pretty-please approach perfected by hip-hop star Missy Elliott. 'Turning your back on the bootleggers helps us pave the way for the next generation of entrepreneurs,' she told the Pro-Music website. 'We do our best to bring you the latest, hottest beats, and we appreciate it when our fans show their love and respect by going in that record store and buying the finished product.'

Herein lies the problem. Rock, pop, punk, techno, rap – all of these genres have in the past challenged the establishment and decried capitalism. 50 years after Bill Haley recorded

'Rock Around The Clock' it seems to many fans that online music is now about capitalism. At least, that's what they tell themselves as they click on the free file-sharer.

Ultimately though, legal downloads will become the norm and the industry will get its cut. There are even signs that the wider market will boost CD sales – up an impressive 9.4 per cent in the US during 2003/04. True, the pirates may never be completely banished but as policing of the Internet gets more sophisticated they'll be navigating stormy waters. Their best chance of survival will be for the suits to seek a cut too much!

In a world where music fans are better informed, better connected and more powerful than ever, that truly would be commercial suicide.

What Is iTunes?

Rather confusingly, iTunes is both the name of the software you use to download music to your iPod and the name of Apple's online music shop where you can actually buy the music to download. Apple recently launched its revolutionary iTunes Music Store in the UK, France and Germany, giving music fans on both sides of the pond the same massive online catalogue, a la carte pricing, free previews, one-click purchasing and downloading, and groundbreaking personal use rights. With Apple's legendary ease of use, pioneering features such as iMix playlist sharing, and breakthrough pricing (just 99 cents in the US, .99 Euro in Germany and France and 79p for the EuroSceptic UK) iTunes is already the number one online music service in the world, and the best way for Mac and PC users to discover and experience their favourite music in an entirely new way. Apple has also announced that it will launch a more complete European Union version of the iTunes Music Store in October 2004 to service the expanding EU.

The iTunes Music Store in the UK, France and Germany all feature over 700,000 songs from all five major music companies and dozens of independent record labels who signed the original agreement, including exclusive tracks from leading worldwide artists such as Anastasia, Ash, The Beastie Boys, Beginner, Black Eyed Peas, The Corrs, Jamie Cullum, The Cure, The Darkness, Arielle Dombasle, Rebel Gilberto, Herbert Groenemeyer, PJ Harvey, The Hives, Indochine, Norah Jones, Keane, Bob Marley, George Michael, Eddy Mitchell, Moby, Pascal Obispo, The Pixies, Rosenstolz, Seeed, Snow Patrol and Mano Solo. The iTunes Music Store will also be releasing a new feature called iTunes Originals which is an in-studio series featuring exclusive recording sessions and interview clips with artists such as Alanis Morissette.

Offering the same ground-breaking personal use rights as in the US, the iTunes Music Store in the UK, France and

Germany gives you the ability to play songs on up to five personal computers, burn a single song onto CDs an unlimited number of times, burn the same playlist up to seven times and listen to their music on an unlimited number of iPods.

iTunes Music Store Features

The iTunes Music Store in the UK, France and Germany offers Mac and PC users the same innovative features including:

- iMix, an innovative tool for publishing playlists of your favourite songs on the iTunes Music Store for other users to preview, rate and purchase. Since iMix creates a virtual iTunes community, it enables users to discover new music recommended by fellow music fans and rate the iMixes published by other iTunes users.

- Party Shuffle, a playlist that automatically chooses songs from your music library, displays just-played and upcoming songs, and allows you to easily add, delete and rearrange upcoming songs on the fly. Party Shuffle is viewed by many as the ultimate DJ at any gathering and a great way for users to get reacquainted with their personal music library. And it doesn't rap over the tracks.

- More than 5,000 audiobooks which can be purchased with one click and listened to on any Mac or Windows computer as well as on iPods. iTunes is the only digital music jukebox that allows you to seamlessly purchase audiobooks in the same easy fashion that you purchase music.

- Instant registration on the iTunes Music Store for AOL Europe customers using existing screen names and passwords with direct links to buy songs from the iTunes Music Store in the UK, France and Germany. Exclusive recordings from Sessions@AOL and AOL's Broadband Rocks will be available on the iTunes Music Store in the UK, France and Germany.

- The ability to create and print stunning CD jewel case inserts for albums or compilation discs, combining album art and track lists using professionally designed templates. For compilation

CDs, iTunes will automatically generate a mosaic of album covers based on the chosen songs.

- Automatic WMA to AAC conversion, enabling Windows users to automatically create iTunes versions of their songs encoded in unprotected WMA. Converting an entire music library into iTunes and syncing it onto iPod is now a snap, even for the Wintel crowd.

iTunes for Mac and Windows includes the iTunes Music Store and is available as a free download immediately from www.apple.com/uk/itunes, www.apple.com/fr/itunes and www.apple.com/de/itunes. Purchase and download of songs from the iTunes Music Store for Mac or Windows requires a valid credit card with a British, French or German billing address. Until politicians decide otherwise, the iTunes Music Store works with the British Pound in the UK and the Euro in France and Germany.

iTunes vs the Record Shop

n the UK, for example, customers can search for songs, hear 30-second previews and buy individual tracks, or a complete album for £7.99, undercutting not only most record shops but supermarkets and online traders as well. As mentioned earlier, all songs can then be burned onto CDs, stored on a Mac or PC computer or placed onto iPods. Since more than 3 million iPods have been sold already, Apple probably has a right to brag that it can't make them fast enough. Out in the traditional money trough, record companies have been hit by a 7.6 per cent fall in retail music sales in 2003 and have reluctantly admitted that the distribution of music has now, well and truly entered the digital age.

While it has been heralded as the end of the record shop, the death of the single and the defeat of online music pirates, Apple's all conquering iTunes music store may find a bit more resistance in Europe than it did after its launch in the US. The music industry, once and continually suspicious of music that exists only as a digital file, rather than as a record or CD, may have reservedly welcomed the arrival of the 'revolutionary' store in Europe. And generally, the industry has expressed hopes that it will persuade millions more people to buy music online, as well as encourage music pirates to purchase what they once obtained freely, but illegally, over the internet. Like it or not, it's good business. Particularly since in a little over a year, 85 million songs have been bought from iTunes in the US, where it has a 70 per cent share of the market in legal downloads. Ironically, music downloading could be the salvation of the outdated *Top Of The Pops* and other chart shows that rely on sales of singles, or a combination of sales and radio airplay to gauge a tracks' popularity. An official download chart is expected to be launched in autumn 2004, as a precursor to digital tracks being included in the official UK Top 40. Record chiefs hope the move will revive the troubled singles chart.

iTunes: the Software

iTunes the software, on the other hand, is still the ultimate jukebox program for the Mac or PC when it comes to things like playing and organising your music, copying music from CDs, burning new CDs the way you want them to sound and generally keeping your iPod full of more music than you'll probably ever have time to listen to.

Back in the last century, at the end of the '90s, the whole MP3 music thing really took off. When iTunes first appeared in 2001, more than 275,000 people downloaded it in the first week. As an all-around music program, iTunes was (and still is) versatile, solid and robust, and particularly easy to use.

Best of all, it was free. Even this early version allowed users to import songs from CDs, convert them to MP3s, play MP3s as well as audio CDs and Internet radio, burn audio CDs without paying for an extra software package and even space out while watching the animated laser-light displays in the iTunes window. When the iPod arrived later that same year, an updated version of iTunes created the perfect match which has enabled this attractive couple to live happily ever after.

Software features
In each reincarnation, iTunes gets better and better. Currently, features include:

- The new AAC format which provides better sound quality while taking up less space.

- The ability to burn your music collection to DVD, which can hold 4.7GB.

- A music sharing feature allowing you to play music from any Mac or PC on any network without any special set-up or configuration.

- Space in the iTunes window to display artwork or images, eg album covers, while you play your songs.

- The ability to save on-the-run playlists made on your iPod while you're home or away.

- A convenient voice-memo facility.

- The ability to create dynamic smart playlists that reflect you preferences or listening habits.

- The ability to customise and save your own settings with each song.

With iTunes, you can copy songs freely to other folders, other discs and other computers – or at least up to three at once.

What Is iPod?

The iPod is decidedly different from any other portable music device to date. Essentially, the iPod is a hard drive that's just too clever by half, cleverly combined with a digital music player in a single compact device. This means it holds considerably more music than other MP3 players and the design is, well – just cool. It weighs less than two CDs and is designed for easy one-handed operation. You can take it just about anywhere since it provides up to 20 minutes of skip protection so the music will play on without missing a beat regardless of how much you personally rock and roll. If all that isn't enough, for the real gadget freaks and mobile phone accessorisors, it also doubles as a portable hard disk back-up and holds boring personal information such as your calendar and address book.

You'll get between 10 and 12 hours of continuous music on three hours of charge. Or, you can fast-charge the battery to 80 per cent capacity in about an hour. The battery recharges automatically through its own power supply or through a Mac or PC connected by a FireWire cable.

tip The bad news is, you can't remove, let alone replace, an iPod battery. When it gives up the ghost, you just have to get a whole new iPod. A full charge takes around four hours. But whatever you do, only use the power adapter supplied by Apple. Anything else will increase your risk of having to buy a whole new unit. Also, always remove the iPod from its carrying case before recharging. The bottom acts as a cooling surface to dissipate the heat. So don't box it in. Incidentally, in response to user complaints about non-replaceable batteries, Apple now offers a battery replacement program and a special AppleCare warranty just for iPods.

What You Get

Like all Apple products, the iPod comes complete with everything you need. Well, apart from the computer, that is. When you unpack it, make sure you've got:

• the CD-ROM containing iTunes software for the Mac and MusicMatch for the PC;

• the necessary cables. Current iPods come with a dock and a special cable to connect the dock to the Mac FireWire connection. Older models provided a FireWire cable for connecting the iPod directly to the computer's FireWire connection.

iPod in dock

- a set of ear-phones;

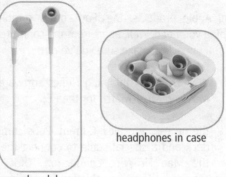

in-ear headphones

headphones in case

- a remote controller (connects to the iPod with wires);

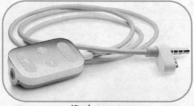

iPod remote

- if you're lucky, a carrying case and some goodies.

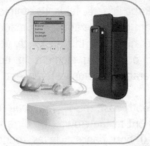

iPod, carrying case, dock, headphones

Why You'll Like It

Apart from its devilish good looks, what makes the iPod so cool? Well, how about this:

- Ease of Use. Like all Apple products, the interface is fantastic. You can get to any song, artist, album or play list in under 3 seconds.

- Sounds Phenomenal. The iPod has a 20–20,000Hz frequency response and Apple has included 18mm Neodymium-magnet transducer headphones to help you enjoy that sound. If you aren't an earwax junkie or audio geek, basically Neodymium (check the Periodic Table; its atomic number is 60), is a rare earth metal used in magnets, lasers and purple glass. In this instance, it emulates the driver, or moving element in normal speakers comparable to a home stereo. And they're white...

- It's Bloody Fast. This is what really makes the iPod stand out in the crowd. The ultra fast FireWire or USB2.0 port dances circles round MP3 players with USB or serial ports. A 4-minute song takes about 1 second to copy onto your iPod with a FireWire connection.

- It's Bloody Tiny. Compared to other large capacity MP3 players, the iPod could almost be completely concealed during a strip search (depending on how adventurous you are...). Big-boned cousins like the Archos's Jukebox HD-MP3 Recorder looks like a microwave oven compared to the iPod.

- Great Memory. Go on – try to fill up the iPod's 30GB drive. I dare you – even if you are a Dead

Head with the ultimate collection of Grateful Dead live bootlegs.

- A Really Hard Hard Drive. Forget lugging around floppy, Zip and Jaz discs around – those days are dead and gone. Connect your iPod and it shows up on your Desktop allowing you to copy practically anything you want onto it. And if all that isn't enough, it's a bootable hard drive. You can even jump start your computer off it if you need to.

- A Display to Make a Peacock Jealous. The iPod has a 2-inch LCD screen capable of displaying all the text associated with your music file, plus, it has a super bright back light.

- Terrific Battery. As mentioned earlier, Apple has equipped the iPod with a rapid recharging 10 hour Lilon battery that charges through the FireWire port when you connect it to your computer to add more songs. Apple also includes an AC adapter for when you don't have your computer around.

- Game for a Laugh. Although I'm not sure this is really a positive feature, there's even a bunch of games to keep you amused while listening to your tunes. Apple has included the classic game Breakout, which apparently is a tribute to one of Apple's early founders, Steve Wozniak, who created and programmed the original arcade version.

OK, so let's assume you've just spent lots of money, bought an iPod and unpacked the box. How the hell do you set it up? Well, it's actually a lot easier than you can imagine.

Setting Up

To begin, unwrap it and plug your iPod into either your FireWire equipped computer or the wall charger. Let it charge for about 3 hours, or until the front of the display shows a fully charged battery in the upper right corner. After that, you're ready to download or sync it to your music collection.

tip

Don't call your iPod "iPod", because then it will always say "Would you like to connect to iPod "iPod", which is very silly indeed.

Syncing your iPod

In order to sync an iPod to your computer, you must have four things:

- a Macintosh or PC;

- a current OS;

- connectors as described earlier;

- iTunes2.0.4 or later.

If you've got all these, you're ready for lift-off. If you're missing any one of them, visit Apple.com.

After you've done that:

1   Open up iTunes.

2   Plug in your iPod to set it up.

You'll have to give it a name (if you screw up, it's easy to rename later). After that, the FireWire kicks in and it downloads all the songs, playlists, and song information into your device.

OK, it's unlikely, but, what if you already have more music than your iPod? Well, you could get a bigger iPod or, if that's not an option, then iTunes will beep at you to indicate that you have too much music, and that it can't automatically sync that much. You can fix this by:

1   putting your favourite songs into a playlist and then only sync that playlist.

2   switching your iPod to manual mode and manually drag the songs you want into it, or

3   you can just sync 'checked songs'.

Notice that on all of your songs, there's a little blue check box to the left. If you uncheck a song, then it won't sync to the iPod. Also note, it won't play in iTunes in shuffle mode. You can double click on it to play as much as you like, but iPod will skip it.

 All of these options can be enabled by clicking the little iPod graphic in the lower-right of your window. Converting all of your songs to .aac files works great too and will reduce the size dramatically on most MP3's you've previously ripped. If you're having

trouble getting your iPod to sync, Apple has a great page of all the tricks to try to fix it, so check them out.

One for the rippers

tip

There's one thing you should switch if you have a lot of music CDs and are planning to rip them onto your computer. It will help save space on your hard drive.

1   Go to the **preferences** menu and

2   go to the 'importing' window

3   from there, choose to import the songs using the .aac convertor.

The files will be much smaller, sound just as good, and if you're really into this sort of thing, possibly even more fun to use.

Listening to your iPod

Obviously, apart from the fashion statement, the most important aspect of your iPod is how it sounds. As mentioned above, the earphones Apple provides are great for music. But if you're looking for greater comfort, try a pair of Sony W-Ear headphones. They're not huge ear-muffs like some headphones, but they still deliver terrific sound.

If you want to listen to your iPod on your stereo, purchase a stereo headphone plug to composite audio cable (composite is that white and yellow and red pronged cord you typically use to connect your TV and VCR and DVD player together). These sound great and are available at a reasonable price from just about every electronics shop around. Another option is to buy a headphone-to-tapedeck adapter if you want to play your iPod in your car.

You might also want to try iTrip, an FM broadcaster that works out of the stereo jack on your iPod. Depending where you are, you can select a few stations, and it will broadcast to your iPod up to 30 feet away. When this works, it's pretty cool. You aren't tethered to your audio system and your iPod impresses the crowd even more. But, it doesn't always work and often, it's hard to find a station that's clear enough. However, it's worth experimenting.

iPod with iTunes

Since they were obviously meant for each other, you'll probably spend most of your time using iTunes with your iPod. While iTunes, like most Apple products, is simple to use, it also has some advanced features. For example, to edit a song's artist or title, or other information, either click on the specific part you want to change or open up the Info (Command i) and change it there. In this Info section you can also change the times of when songs start and stop. If you want to edit multiple items, select them while holding shift (select all between two points) or while holding command (select the ones you pick), and use Get Info or Command i to change them. This is useful if the artist changes their name, and you want to update all of their songs.

129

tip To turn the backlight on, hold down the menu button for a few seconds. It will go off automatically after about 30 seconds.

Essentially, the iPod-related parts are pretty simple. When you plug in your iPod, iTunes starts and syncs it. You can press the little iPod in the lower left of the iTunes window to play with options since it's set to sync everything automatically. iPod also lets you sync specific playlists. You can turn on 'Manual Mode' if you want to drag and drop songs to the iPod. The 'FireWire Disk Mode' can be used to stick other stuff on your iPod like documents and files.

While iTunes 4.5 lets you share all your songs with friends on a local network, your might find that some tracks pop up a dialogue on other users' computers. As you will gather, the only limitations on songs come from the iTunes Music Store and are by far, the least strict you will find on any legal site. Songs downloaded from the Music Store can be put on your iPod, burned as much as you like – that limitten-playlist thing is about stopping people from buying commercial CDs and then copying them over and over and selling them – and shared on up to three computers.

Whomever you share the music with needs to have your password for the iTunes Music Store. So, the only catch is that you need to be rather careful about who you give this to because once they have your password, they are free to do whatever they want with your music.

 tip To reset your iPod, hold down the menu and play buttons for 5 seconds until the Apple Logo Appears. Unfreezing won't erase your songs.

Your iPod Settings

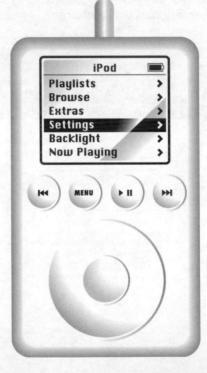

Briefly, the sorts of things you'll find in the settings dialogue are things like:

- Shuffle: which picks a random order to play all your songs. It has two modes: On/Off

- Repeat: Repeats a certain song, or everything; three modes: One (Current Track) /All/Off

133

- Backlight Timer: Default setting On/Off, but what it does is turns on the backlight every time you touch a button or wheel. You can select between 1-5 seconds, or just have it on all the time.

- EQ - Bass Booster: An Apple iTunes option to equalise all the sound volumes from songs...nice, but uses up loads of battery. It has two modes: On/Off

- Sound Check: An equaliser that runs through lots of preset EQ settings for adjusting the bass and treble to sound better. Works great, but uses shed-loads of battery power.

- Contrast: You can set the contrast if you feel the screen is too dark or light. Usually plenty bright.

- Clicker. Is the audible click you hear whenever you scroll with the wheel. By the way, the iPod has a speaker for that so it doesn't come out of your headphones. You can turn it off if you don't like it.

- Language: Yes, you can even use your iPod in another language...

- Reset all Settings.

Extras

Clock

- Alarm Clock: Wake up the rock 'n' roll way...

- Sleep Timer: Turns the iPod off after a set period of time, even while playing music. Great if you like to fall asleep to music, but you don't want the iPod to play it to you while you're sleeping. You can set it to between 5 minutes and one hour.

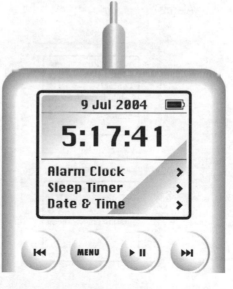

Calendar

iPod Calendar features include:

- All: This opens up a monthly calendar on your iPod, where you can select a given day and enter an appointment or other important reminder

- To Do

- Alarms

How Much Does It All Cost?

If you haven't already bought yourself an iPod, I would imagine you've talked yourself into one by now. So the next thing you probably want to know is, how much does all this cost? At the time of writing, the iPod starts at £249 in the UK and $299 in the US and the iPod Mini starts at $249 in the US, with release in the UK scheduled in the fall of 2004. Check out Apple's web site for full pricing details on iPods and accessories as well. It's probably worth shopping around, but new iPods will probably be priced quite consistently in each country they're available in. A few second-hand iPods are finding their way onto market so sites like eBay might also be worth a look. Sure, it's always worth buying a new iPod for all sorts of reasons, but one of the reasons for buying it in the first place is that it's well made and will continue to function well for a long time. So, if you find a low-mileage iPod at a good price, don't be afraid to go for it. After all, if it ain't baroque, don't fix it.

Creating a Music Directory

As a rather dour alternative comedian used to say, 'You can't have everything. Where would you put it?'. Blessed with an iTunes library that can hold an awesome 32,000 songs, depending on available disk space, finding your favourite song amidst the musical equivalent of the British Library can, initially, appear to be a rather daunting task. And since even the smaller 40Gb iPod can hold up to 9,000 songs (which would still last you two weeks even if you played it 24 hours a day) you're obviously going to want to impose some order on your collection. Like any library or collection, you'll need to know how to search, browse and sort all those tunes so you can easily locate any artist, album, music genre or other classification you choose quickly and easily.

Let's face it. Even if we don't take into account the amount of music you can acquire from your own CD collection and other sources, your online sources for music downloads gets more formidable by the day. And, there's plenty of evidence that users are taking full advantage of those options. For instance, in the first week after its European launch, music lovers in the UK, France and Germany purchased and downloaded more than 800,000 songs from the iTunes Music Store, with more than 450,000 sold in the UK alone –16 times as many as its closest competitor, OD2.

But once you start acquiring all this music, how do you manage it? Fortunately, both iTunes and the iPod provide a variety of facilities for building playlists of songs and albums, browsing your music library, changing viewing options, searching for songs and artists and automatically updating your song information.

iTunes Library

Although the iPod and iTunes are particularly easy to get up and running and you'll have probably already downloaded loads of songs before you start wondering how to manage them, one of the first useful things you need to figure out is exactly where your music library is. Sure, your music is relatively safe and secure. But like any computer or portable storage device, Buffy-style demons will always be lurking in the shadows waiting for an opportunity to wreak havoc on your collection. And like any digital device, cigarette ash in your keyboard or an iPod accidentally dropped off a seaside pier can spell disaster for your meticulously acquired music collection. That's why, as with any computer system, back-ups are important – particularly if you've downloaded some rare or particularly unusual music that doesn't exist anywhere else in your current non-virtual reality tunnel.

Like it or not, you won't be able to copy your music files from your iPod to your Mac or PC without using a third-party program. The problem? Apple doesn't support any of the third-party options. So, the best bet is to keep a back-up of your iTunes Library on your Mac or PC and don't rely exclusively on your iPod as your music storage device.

You can also treat your iPod as a FireWire hard drive to copy music or any other files back and forth from your Mac or PC. The only problem is, when it comes to music files, you won't be able to find them because the iPod uses a music management database that's essentially invisible. The name of this phantom folder is 'iPod Control' and there are loads of utilities for both the Mac and PC that will make it visible and mess-aroundable.

tip If you're careless enough to drag the iTunes Music folder to a different location without properly informing iTunes, the next time you start the program it will appear to be empty. Don't Panic! Just remember to always let iTunes know where you're moving it:

1   choose iTunes Preferences on the Mac or Edit Preferences on Windows
2   click on the Advanced tab
3   find the area called iTunes Music Folder Location

4   click the Change button, and
5   indicate the place where you've moved it
6   click OK.

Fortunately, iTunes is a great tool for eliminating chaos in your music file storage. You can install it anywhere and iTunes always remembers its own location and folder.

Finding Your Music

Inside your iTunes folder is another iTunes Music folder and all the songs you import or download will be stored here. Even if you drag files to the iTunes window, iTunes will automatically make a copy and store that copy in the Music folder. If you want to find the location of any song:

1   select the song

2   choose Get Info from your File menu bar and

3   click the Info tab in the Song Information window

4   in the Summary pane, look in the Kind section and the Where section will tell you exactly where the song is.

Song Information

Crying

| Info | Tags | Options |

Kind: MPEG audio file	**Format:** MPEG-1, Layer 3
Time: 4:50	**Bit Rate:** 160 kbps
Size: 5.6 MB	**Sample Rate:** 44.100 kHz
Date Modified: 11/11/03 11:17 am	**Channels:** Joint Stereo
Play Count: 1	**ID3 Tag:** v2.2
Last Played: 16/6/04 5:13 pm	**Encoded by:** iTunes v3.0.1
Where: Iain's Data:Users:admin: Music:iTunes:iTunes Music:Bjork:Debut:02 Crying.mp3	

Despite its cool exterior, the soul lurking inside iTunes is nothing more than an extremely powerful database with attitude. Its job is simply to search, sort, display and otherwise manage your music information in a fast, precise manner. And, it happens to be bloody good at its job. It allows you to create your own personalised directories or playlists of particular songs that you've decided should go together. How you choose to group, arrange or order songs is totally up to you.

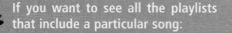
If you want to see all the playlists that include a particular song:

1   press the Control key and click the song,
2   scroll down to Playlists.

You can also open a playlist in its own window by double-clicking the playlist's name. iTunes opens the playlist in a new window and switches its main window to the Library view. You can open as many playlist windows as you like, and drag songs between them. It's a handy way to work, since it lets you see the contents of your Library and your playlist at the same time.

Creating a Playlist

To create a playlist either:

1   press Apple+N on the Mac or Ctrl+N on a Windows PC

2   choose File and then New Playlist

3   click the + button under the Source area of the iTunes window.

After you've created and named the playlist, you've got two methods for adding songs. Either:

1   drag your songs from your Library window to your Playlist window or

2   drag them over from the Songs window and drop them on the Playlist's icon in the Source list.

tip Here's a shortcut for creating a playlist:

1 in the Library view, **select the songs you want to include in a playlist**

☑ Symphony No.5 in C minor (All...	5:34	Beethoven	The
☑ Bagatelle in A minor, Wo023 (F...	3:09	Beethoven	The
☑ Symphony No.3 in E flat major ...	5:56	Beethoven	The
☑ Piano sonata No.8 in C minor (...	4:46	Beethoven	The
☑ Violin Concerto in D major	11:16	Beethoven	The
☑ Piano sonata No.14 in C sharp ...	5:19	Beethoven	The
☑ Symphony No.6 in F major (Pas...	11:05	Beethoven	The
❶ ☑ Piano Concerto No.5 (Emperor)	10:03	Beethoven	The
☑ Overture to Egmont	8:25	Beethoven	The
☑ Symphony No.9 in D minor (Ch...	13:51	Beethoven	The
☑ It Could Have Been a Brilliant C...	2:23	Belle & Sebastian	The
☑ Sleep The Clock Round	4:58	Belle & Sebastian	The
☑ Is It Wicked Not To Care?	3:22	Belle & Sebastian	The

2 choose **New Playlist From Selection** from the File menu.

File	Edit	Controls	Visuals	Advanced
New Playlist				⌘N
New Playlist From Selection				⇧⌘N
New Smart Playlist...				⌥⌘N
Add to Library...				⌘O
Close Window				⌘W
Import...				⇧⌘O
Export Song List...				
Export Library...				
Get Info...				⌘I
Show Song File				⌘R
Show Current Song				⌘L
Burn Playlist to CD				
Update Songs on "administrator's iPod"				

iTunes will add the songs to a new playlist, which you can then rename.

If you use this second method and already have lots of playlists, just make sure you drop them on the right icon.

Once you've got a playlist, you can change the order of songs by dragging the titles up or down within the Playlist window and you can also drag additional songs into the playlist or delete songs you don't want anymore.

Deleting a playlist
To delete a playlist, select it in the Source list and press Delete or Backspace. This will only remove the playlist, not your actual songs in the library.

Smart Playlists
Although random playlists are good, Smart Playlists can be even better. If you wish, you can have iTunes compose custom playlists all by itself. All you have to do is provide some guidelines and Smart Playlist will rummage around your Music Library and come up with its own mix. It will even keep an eye on the music that comes and goes from your Library and update and adjust itself automatically. You give iTunes whatever detailed instructions you like about selecting artists, genres, years and composers, and you can make a Smart Playlist based on information taken from any field in the song's tag.

To initiate a Smart Playlist, press Option-Apple-N on the Mac or Ctrl+Alt+N on a Windows PC, or just choose New Smart Playlist from the File menu.

 tip Deleting a song from a playlist doesn't really delete it from your Music Library. All it does is remove the title from the playlist.

If you really want to get rid of a song for good, press Delete or Backspace when the Library icon is selected and it will vanish for real. To delete a selected playlist and bypass the confirmation dialogue, hold down Command + Delete.

When you press the Option key on the Mac or the Shift key on a Windows PC, the + button for Add New Playlist at the bottom of the iTunes window transforms into a gear icon. When you engage this gear, you'll get a new Smart Playlist appearing in the Source list and you can set it up however you like. If you leave the Live updating box checked, iTunes will always keep your playlist updated as you add or delete songs to your collection or change the information or ratings on songs that already exist.

Compilations

If you happen to have some compilation CDs in your music collection that aren't too embarrassing, you can get iTunes to store the MP3 files for compilations in a separate folder within your iTunes Music folder. This will help reduce folder chaos and make it easier to locate and manage your MP3 files. For example, say you have a compilation CD that contains tracks from a dozen or so different artists. Normally, iTunes creates a separate folder for each artist - even though that folder might contain just one MP3 file. But if you designate those songs as being part of a compilation, iTunes will store all of those tracks together in their own folder.

To tell iTunes that a song is part of a compilation:

1   select the song

2   choose Get Info from the File menu or press command-I

Song Information

| Info | Tags | Options |

Artist	Year
Otis Redding	2003
Composer	Track Number
	1 of 15
Album	Disc Number
Raw Soul	1 of 1
Comments	

Genre
Blues/R&B ☑ Part of a compilation

Prev Song   Next Song   Cancel   OK

3   in the Tags area of the Song Information window,
       check the Part of a Compilation box.

As with other tag-editing tasks, you can do this for multiple
songs at once by selecting them all before choosing Get
Info. It will come as no surprise that iTunes stores
compilations within a folder whose name is, you guessed it,
Compilations and within this folder, iTunes creates a
separate folder for each compilation you've specified.

Playlists in MusicMatch Jukebox for Windows

While it's my own opinion that iTunes is all the software you'll ever need for downloading and managing your music on both the Mac and PC, there will be some users that either choose or need to use MusicMatch Jukebox with their iPods. As mentioned earlier on, older PCs that can't run Windows 2000 or XP won't be able to use iTunes. Other users may already have an extensive music library in MusicMatch Jukebox and be reluctant to change. As it happens, MusicMatch also has its own online store selling legal music downloads. Unfortunately, as these files are all copy-protected using Windows Media Audio format, you won't be able to play them on your iPod.

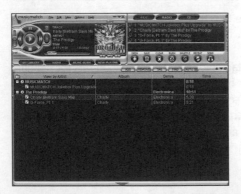

Like iTunes, MusicMatch Jukebox is also nothing more than a jumped-up database and it's capable of doing most of the same things described above for iTunes. In the upper right-hand corner of the MusicMatch screen is the Playlist window. Once this is open, you can do most of the same things described above for iTunes.

- You can drag album titles or performers from the first column in Folder View into the Playlist window.

- You can Right-click a track and choose Add Track(s) from the shortcut menu, or

- you can drag sound files from your desktop or folder windows directly into the Playlist window.

However, if you use this last method, your songs won't get added automatically to the Library unless you change your Preferences.

Changing your Preferences
You can do this by:

1   choosing Settings from the Options menu

2   clicking the General tab

3   where it says 'When double-clicking local music
     files', turn on the Add to Music Library function.

Don't move your original music folders or files around on your hard-drive once you've created playlists. It confuses Windows and you'll have to redo all your playlists again.

Modifying MusicMatch playlists

To modify your playlists in MusicMatch Jukebox:

1   open the Playlist window and click Open. The Open Music dialogue will appear

2   click the Playlists icon on the left side of the box

3   click the name of the particular playlist you want
         to edit or modify

4   click Play to load the tracks into the Playlist
         window and then you can drag the titles up or
         down within the Playlist window to re-organise
         them, delete them or add new songs

5   when you're happy with your mix, click Save.

Deleting playlists in MusicMatch
Now for the weird bit. If you want to delete a playlist:

1   open the Playlist dialogue box

2   click the playlist name and then

3   click Save

4   in the Save Playlist box, click the name of the
     particular one you want to dump

5   click Delete.

Now you see why I heartily recommend using iTunes.

iPod Playlists On-The-Go

Generally, except for On-The-Go playlists, you'll make most
of your playlists on your Mac or PC using iTunes or
MusicMatch Jukebox. Once you've made your various
playlists and synchronised your computer with your iPod,
the whole lot is transferred as you made it to your iPod.
Every playlist you create in iTunes or MusicMatch Jukebox

will appear in the iPod Playlist menu. All you need to do is select the one you want to listen to and press Play. However, you can't modify or delete a playlist on the iPod itself. For that, you've got to go back to iTunes of MusicMatch Jukebox – unless, of course, you decide to use Playlists On-The-Go.

To use the Playlists On-The-Go feature:

1   scroll through your iPod's Music Library and select the song you want to add.

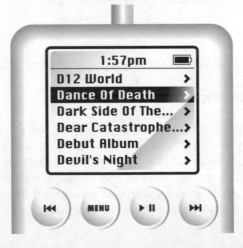

2   Hold down the Select button until the song's title
      blinks three times. This means that it's just been
      added to a special modifiable playlist called,
      appropriately enough, On-The-Go.

tip If you plan to transfer your playlists to an iPod, there's a trick you can use to ensure that a given playlist will appear at the top of the iPod's Playlist menu. It seriously cuts down on the time and scrolling required to find a specific playlist. Just precede the playlist's name with a hyphen (-) character, as in - Mac's Greatest Hits. A few other punctuation characters, including period (.), will also send a playlist to the top of the heap.

Once you've selected a song and added it to the playlist, you can continue to scroll to more songs and add them as well. As well as individual songs, you can also press and select entire albums, artists or even other playlists that you may have made earlier and add them to your On-The-Go compilation.

Once you've created an On-The-Go Playlist, scroll to the bottom of the Playlist menu and press Select to see your new list or press Play to listen to it. Incidentally, early versions of this feature only held songs in its memory until the next time you connected to your computer. Version 2.1 or later of the iPod system software fixes that inconvenience and now lets you sync these spontaneous mixes back into iTunes. That's another good reason why it's always a good idea to ensure you have the latest versions of system software both for your computer and your iPod.

Buying Tunes Online: The Basics

As you've probably gathered by now, the iTunes Music Store features hundreds of thousands of songs from major music companies, including BMG, EMI, Sony Music Entertainment, Universal and Warner Bros, and loads of tracks from independent artists and record labels as well. You'll also find many exclusive tracks from such artists as The Darkness, Jamie Cullum and George Michael, to name just a few.

In the UK, it is now ridiculously easy to quickly find, purchase and download the music you want, when you want it, for a very reasonable 79p (or 99 cents) per song and as little as £7.99/$9.99 per album. You can burn individual songs onto an unlimited number of CDs for your personal use, listen to songs on an unlimited number of iPods and play songs on up to five Macs or Windows PCs. And best of all, the iTunes software works so smoothly on both platforms that you can share music with any combination of Macs and Windows PCs on a local area network, regardless of whether you're running iTunes on a Mac or a PC.

You can browse and shop by genres, such as Rock, Jazz, Latin, New Age, Folk, Opera, R&B/Soul, Reggae and Blues, or by artist or album. All your really need to do is double-click on track listings to hear 30-second, high-quality samples and to see digital album art, or, you can search by entering the name of an artist or composer, the title of a song, or even part of the title. Then, simply click the Search button. Or even easier, just click a Quick Link on an artist in your library and you'll be presented with the band's entire repertoire. When you find something you like, buy it instantly or save the store preview in a playlist on your Mac or PC.

Buying online is also a great way to discover new music and expand your taste. The iTunes Music Store features great editorial content, complete with links to music and you can drag and create links to any store page or share your new-found favourites with friends by emailing them a link to an artist or album page that includes sound samples. Even better, you can share the playlists you make as an iMix on the store. You can also rate playlists from other music lovers to move them up and down the charts and discover whether you rate as a five-star music mixer.

If you have a broadband connection, you can check out exclusive full-length music videos that you can watch right in the store. If you like what you see, just buy the tune immediately. Or, you can check out the latest movie trailers in full screen and buy songs from the soundtrack or an associated audiobook, which is something I probably haven't mentioned yet. For the more literate among you, iTunes even includes a well-stocked library of over 5000 best-selling audiobooks. So, the bottom line is, the iTunes Music Store offers everything you need to build your music collection with ease, give music to friends and family, and expand your musical knowledge in the process.

The Store also helps you keep abreast of what's happening on the music scene and various top songs and top albums are listed on the home page to let you know what's hot and what's not. OK, maybe you won't agree with all the choices, but it's still an interesting point of reference. You'll also find top download lists and related music suggestions scattered throughout the store, designed to help you discover and explore all genres and aspects of an eclectic range of new music.

Shopping on iTunes

When you're ready to go shopping:

1   open iTunes on your computer and

2   click the Music Store icon.

Make sure you're actually connected to the Internet and as you've probably gathered, the whole Store works a lot better over high-speed connections.

After you've clicked the Store icon and made the connection, you'll find yourself on the home page. You'll use the usual iTunes controls to browse, search and select within the Store exactly the same way you would if you were wandering around one of your own iTunes Music Libraries.

Opening an Apple Account

If you've got the headroom on your credit card and feel like moving forward, the first thing you'll need to do is set up your Apple Account. As usual, this is a simple process:

1   click the Account Sign In button on the right side
     of the iTunes window and

Sign In to buy music on the iTunes Music Store
To create an Apple Account, click Create New Account.

(Create New Account)

If you have an Apple Account (from the Apple Store or .Mac, for example), enter your Apple ID and password. Otherwise, if you are an AOL member, enter your AOL screen name and password.

Apple ID:
                                          Example: steve@mac.com
Password:
                                          (Forgot Password?)

(?)   (Cancel) (Sign In)

2   click the Create New Account button.

(If you happen to be an AOL subscriber, you can by-pass the Apple Account and sign into the Store with your AOL screen name and password.) Although some of you may have already noticed, if you've ever bought or registered any Apple product on the company's web site or perhaps, signed up for AppleCare tech-support, you'll probably already have an Apple ID and all you need to do is remember your user-name and password.

There are then three steps to follow when setting up your account:

1   agreeing usual terms and conditions for using the
        Store and buying music

2   creating your actual Apple Account, and

3   supplying a credit card number and billing address.

The agreement is designed to inform you of your rights and responsibilities as an iTunes customer; once you read through it, click the Agree button and move on. The next screen you'll encounter will ask you to create a user name, password, and some sort of secret question and answer. The question and answer bit is to ensure that if you happen to forget your password, you'll be able to prove to Apple who you are and verify your identity. Probably the most important bit, from a sheerly practical point of view, is the provision of a valid credit card number.

Once you've done all this, from then on, when you want to shop, all you need to do is click the Account Sign In button and you're off and running.

Browsing and downloading

Once you're in the store, Apple provides a one-click option that allows you to download any selected track instantly as soon as you click the Buy Song button. If you've got a high-speed Internet connection, this is a quick and convenient option. However, if you've got a dial-up connection, sitting and waiting for each individual song to download can feel akin to watching the proverbial paint dry. So, like most other Internet retailers, the iTunes Store provides a virtual Shopping Cart that you can push around, fill with goodies, and then check out when you've finished your shopping. When you finish your session, simply click the Shopping Cart icon in the iTunes Source list and choose Buy Now. That way, all your gear is bagged and sent off at once and you can smoke a fag or have a coffee while you download.

Finding what you want, or even finding out where to find what you might want in the iTunes Store is probably easier than browsing in your local high street record shop. There's a pop-up menu in the upper left hand corner of the Store where you can leap straight to the genres of your choice, or randomly select a genre you'd like to find out more about. Once you've chosen a particular genre, iTunes lists all of the artists in the Store that fall into that category. You've also got access to a particularly powerful Power Search tool for getting more specific about artists, albums, songs, genres or composers. If, for example, you choose a band or performer that takes your fancy, simply clicking the name will reveal all the songs and albums in-stock and available for purchase. Clicking on the album name will also list all the songs available from it in the Details window. If you're not familiar with the music, you can then double-click a track and listen to a 30-second sample to decide if it's something you'd really like to purchase.

Strolling around the iTunes Store is essentially like using any other Web browser and most of the songs and artists are hyperlinked so you can check out stuff like album covers or images as well. While you're wandering about, you can always click the Back button to retrace your steps or click on the small house to return to the iTunes Store homepage.

There's loads of other miscellaneous information as well, such as display links to new releases, a list of 'exclusive' stuff that can only be purchased from the iTunes Store, sneak peaks and a searchable Billboard Top 100 Chart list that goes back to 1946. A lot of the musicians in the Featured Artists section offer a range of free videos that you can watch while in iTunes – if your connection is fast enough or you don't mind paying the phone bill.

Making your purchase
When you get to the end of your shopping spree and decide to click the Buy button, make sure you really want to purchase all the songs or albums you've selected. Out in

cyberspace, all sales are final and there's no real facility for returning unwanted downloads. You will get the usual alert asking you to confirm or cancel your purchases before proceeding. But if you've got more money then sense and don't really care what you spend it on, you can always click the 'Don't warn me about buying songs' option and you'll never see the confirmation box again.

> **tip** When you download a video, iTunes will unfortunately stop playing other songs you may have selected. However, you can get round this by double-clicking the song in the Source window to open it in a separate window. This will allow you to listen to your chosen music while iTunes works away in the background downloading your video.

Non-music Options in iTunes

Audiobooks

You can choose and purchase a range of audiobook titles from the iTunes Store. The iPod is compatible with Audible.com's own electronic books format which includes various spoken word titles, books and newspapers. These are primarily the sort of audio books you can purchase from the iTunes Store. Although you're probably wondering how you might preview this selection as you are unable to cut and paste the entire text without paying, there is an equivalent solution to the 30-second sound sample already on offer.

The iTunes Store offers both a description of the book's content and something called a Sonic Preview which gives you 90 seconds to skim the title before deciding to buy it. When you buy an audiobook, it comes straight through iTunes in an iPod-friendly format – which is more than happens when you buy the same titles directly from Audible's own site.

Gift certificates

For those of you who are terrible at remembering things like birthdays, anniversaries and holidays, and always find that by the time you remember, the shops are closed and you're destined for an ear-bashing or the serious cold-shoulder routine, then the iTunes Shop Gift Certificates could be a life-saver. These handy little numbers are available from the iTunes Store or directly from Apple's web site and the process of buying them is more or less as explained above for buying anything else on the web. Since you can purchase Gift Certificates anytime, anywhere, you can always get yourself out of trouble by saying that you didn't really forget – your present is in your email.

The other advantage of this scheme is that redemption is only a click away and the Redeem Now button lets you type in the confirmation number printed on the lower edge of the actual Gift Certificate. There's also an Allowance Account scheme available through the iTunes Store which allows you to allocate a certain amount of money to a particular account that can then be spent, but only up to the limit you set. And, if you happen to forget how much money you have left on either your Gift Certificate or Allowance Account, don't panic. The balance will always appear right next to your account name in the iTunes window.

> **tip** A quick way to check out recently added songs at the iTunes Store is to click on the Just Added link found on the left side of the main Music Store page. Further down, you find additional information on what celebrities are listening to so that you can have a listen as well.

The Competition: The World of MP3s

Napster

If you spend much time online, particularly looking for music to download, then you have most likely heard of Napster. What began in 1999 as an idea in the head of a teenager proceeded to redefine the Internet, the music industry and the way we all think about intellectual property. Napster is now back in business as a legal, pay-per-song music-download site. But it once was a controversial service that scared the hell out of the record industry and spurred what is still one of the greatest Internet-related debates. If we can get the music we want without paying for it – why should we?

OK, so the first people to discover the potential of the Internet for downloading music were branded as pirates. And, because they were able to deliver such a good service, modern-day legal services have been forced to offer a much better product at increasingly competitive prices to lure users away from pirate sites.

In early 1999, Shawn Fanning began to develop an idea as he talked with friends about the difficulties of finding the kind of MP3 files they were interested in. He thought that there should be a way to create a program that combined three key functions into one. These functions are:

- Search engine: Dedicated to finding MP3 files only

- File sharing: The ability to trade MP3 files directly, without having to use a centralised server for storage

- Internet Relay Chat (IRC): A way to find and chat with other MP3 users while online.

Napster was Fanning's nickname in high school, because of his hair, and even In its present incarnation, it offers a different way to distribute MP3 files. Instead of storing the songs on a central computer, the songs live on users' machines. This is called peer-to-peer sharing, or P2P. When you want to download a song using Napster, you are downloading it from another person's machine, and that person could be your next-door neighbour or someone halfway around the world.

The problem that the music industry had with Napster was that it was a big, automated way to copy copyrighted material. It is a fact that thousands of people were, via

Napster, making thousands of copies of copyrighted songs, and neither the music industry nor the artists got any money in return for those copies. And, despite the plethora of industry-approved legal sites emerging, this type of piracy is still happening now, through sites other than Napster. This is why there was so much emotion around it. Many people loved Napster because they could get music for free instead of paying shop prices for a CD. The music industry was against Napster because people could get music for free instead of paying, what many conside to be inflated and manipulated prices for a CD. Napster's defence was that the files were personal files that people maintained on their own machines, and therefore Napster was not responsible.

Individuals have always tended to be less concerned about copyright laws than businesses have to be, so individuals continue to make all sorts of copyrighted songs available to the world from their personal machines. This means, in theory, that anyone can download for free, any song that someone has taken the time and effort to encode in the MP3 format. Other file-sharing services such as Kazaa and Soulseek still let you download music for free. But, the view here is that you would be breaching copyright law and the music industry takes a sour view of anything like this and have endeavoured to target persistent offenders.

Probably the biggest question that most people have about Napster and other free music services is, 'How did they make money?' The short answer is simply, 'They didn't.' Initially, Napster was never intended to be a revenue-generating business. Like many other such services, one view is that if you've already bought a CD, it's yours and if you want to make a copy of it, you should be entitled to do it. Another view, from just plain music lovers, is that making a wide range of music available for free will actually encourage people to go out and buy the real thing in, say, the form of a CD. And, like many great inventors before, Shawn Fanning created his original program just to see if it could be done – not because of money. But even he had no idea how big this whole phenomenon would become.

However, after some time away, Napster is now back in a legal permutation, offering over 50,000 tracks at 99p each, or £10 for an album. Software can be quite large at around 7Mb and downloading it can take over 20 minutes on a dial-up modem. Search times are almost immediate and download time is competitive. However, there are a lot of famous omissions, such as the Beatles and Harry Potter, and the software provided doesn't always work with all computers.

Other MP3 services

And Napster is not the only one out there. Digital music has come a long way in the past year and even the record industry has at last woken up to the biggest revolution in our listening and buying habits since the introduction of CDs. Today, it's increasingly possible to download your music direct from the label or licensed retailer - for free or at a price. Some of the other services out there include:

OD2

OD2, founded by former Genesis front man Peter Gabriel, is the outfit behind most of the UK's major digital download retailers. Having signed deals with all five major record labels and some indies, it handles the technology and licensing for the following high-profile stores – allowing users to download tracks on a pay-as-you-go basis.

Amazon

This services offers a selection of downloadable tracks from high-profile artists, from the online retailing behemoth. For the moment at least, it's free and Amazon is either trying to drive traffic before it starts charging, or hopes its downloads will push up CD sales. Musicians are encouraged to upload MP3s.

Artist Direct

A similar model to Amazon where users can download selected free tracks from high-profile artists, in MP3 or Windows Media, courtesy of the record label. (Currently a US-only site.)

Virgin Megastore

The site is browser-based and works in a similar fashion to Amazon or Play.com. There's no software to download and you just type in your credit card details. You've got a choice of around 350,000 songs and search times can be over 30 seconds. Download time is slightly longer than some other sites and tracks are downloaded in WMA format, which unfortunately, isn't compatible with all MP3 players. There's no Beatles or Harry Potter here either, but tracks only cost 99p.

EMusic

Subscription-based service that allows users to download a limited number of MP3s for £9.99 or $14.99 a month. Available worldwide, it has a good esoteric selection, but most of the best-known artists are often absent.

Epitonic

Another free site for legal downloads in WMA or MP3 – so long as they're for personal use. The music is by independent or underground artists, but US artists tend to dominate the scene. It provides personalised radio which allows you to choose from a wide variety of genres, select how many tracks you want to hear, and they do the rest. Smart editorial and a well-organised site make this well worth a look and listen if you want to expand your musical horizons.

Insound

A vast collection of free indie MP3s from an online shop selling CDs and gig tickets to a US market only.

MyCokeMusic.com

Probably one of the most high-profile online music stores, MyCokeMusic.com is just one of a number of retailers using the OD2 system. Noteworthy for the fact that a drinks manufacturer is diversifying into online music.

Playlouder

This is a UK music site whose design comes in two versions: loud and louder. You can join the 'singles club' for free downloads of three selected bands a month, buy digital singles from featured artists for £1.50 to £2, or go to an OD2-driven download shop for a wider selection of tracks.

Streets Online

Streets Online is a UK digital music store owned by Woolworths. It was launched as a commercial download service in November 2003. Its beta version offers albums at £7.99 and single tracks at 99p, but the range is extremely limited.

Trax2Burn

A specialist service that sells MP3s from three house music labels: End Recordings, Underwater and FatBoy Slim's Southern Fried. Individual tracks are the only things available and cost 99p each.

Vitaminic.com

This Pan-European site offers unlimited access to a wide range of music for $69.99 (£38.49) a year, or $39.99 (£21.99) for six months. It also contains fairly unique sections with opportunities for unsigned artists to promote their work.

Label-based services

A lot of record companies have begun to see the writing on

the wall and have launched their own online services for downloading music. Some of these in the UK include:

Matador
This lot proved free MP3s featuring tracks from bands such as Pavement, Mogwai and Pretty Girls Make Graves.

Subpop
The classic indie label whose back catalogue includes Afghan Whigs and Nirvana – but downloads, though free, are only available for more recent signings such as The Shins and Rosie Thomas.

Virgin Records
Branson's pickle offers free 'sneaky peeks' of tracks from the Virgin Records label, which is now nothing to do with Virgin Megastore, plus high-profile, new singles for a fee.

Warp Records
This London-based indie label has made its back catalogue and releases available directly online as MP3 downloads. Tracks cost 99p.

The record industry has started backing legal services and many have already launched, or are at least toying with the idea of launching, their own versions of what iTunes already does so well. Keep an eye out for the launch of a definitive online chart in September 2004 – but don't lose site of the opportunities offered by many of these services to explore and promote new, original and creative style music.

Creating Your Own Music – and Listening to It

Although the bulk of the music you'll probably be listening to on your iPod will come from the iTunes Store or other music downloads, you can also utilise iTunes to create your own music or compile music from other existing sources. We've already discussed some basics regarding system requirements and the like, but perhaps it's worthwhile having a slightly more in-depth look at the more arcane inner-workings of your Mac with iTunes.

Using Mac OSX

Mac OS X version 10.3, otherwise know as 'Panther', gives you just about everything you need to live in the digital age. The entire system and its applications are designed to work well with each other and and particularly, to suit your individual computing style. Critically-acclaimed applications let you organise and create digital media with elegant simplicity and a complete suite of Internet software offers you intuitive communications capabilities. And Apple's typically elegant built-in tools let you be productive immediately. The latest version of Mac OS X also provides a luscious, liquid interface, called Aqua, across every application and the utilities you need to control and customise your Mac. Plus, you can easily connect your Mac to any network, whether wired or wireless, Mac-, UNIX- or Windows-based. Best of all, it just works.

Essentially, OS X on a Mac really lets you do fun, creative things with your pictures, music and movies in ways that PC users can only dream about. For example, you can make movies and share them via email, the Web or on DVD. You can organise your digital pictures into albums and set your desktop to play from any iPhoto album. You can share your iTunes playlist with other Macs and PCs in the house with zero configuration Rendezvous, mix CDs for friends, download songs from the iTunes Store, play DVDs on the road or at home while taking advantage of DVDs with expanded Web content, and, if the rumours are correct, it won't be long before you'll be able to play videos on your iPod.

What it lets you do
Mac OS X includes all the applications you need to access and use the Internet immediately with no fuss – and the simple and elegant design is easy to use and intuitive for new users, while still including a plethora of powerful features for professionals. With little or no effort you can:

*   Navigate open windows quickly with Expos.

*   Animate your desktop picture with iPhoto albums.

*   Use a graphics tablet to input text in English, French or German.

*   Get quick access to frequent file commands in the new pop-up Actions menu.

*   Compress/expand files directly in the Finder.

* Search for files with iTunes-like speed and ease.

* Assign colour labels with customised names to any file or folder.

* Switch to another User Account without logging out and quitting current applications.

* Access Help instruction via purple help icons.

* Customise keyboard shortcuts for the System and applications.

* View active application icons semi-transparently, heads-up style when using Command-Tab.

* Install fonts by clicking single button in Font Book.

* Use OpenGL-enhanced screen effects when your Mac is idle, then require a password to wake up.

* See misspelled words as you type in many applications, including Mail, iChat and TextEdit.

* Use Preview, the world's fastest PDF reader, which

renders PDFs three times faster than Windows.

* Build automatic PDF indexes from your searches.

* Use dozens of high-quality fonts included with Panther.

* Wake from sleep instantly, with optional password verification.

* Secure the contents of your home directory with powerful AES-128 encryption.

* Control which applications your kids can use.

* Make your Mac easier to use if you have difficulties which includes iSight and iChat AV for long distance sign language.

Other special features
Other useful features in Panther let you use your digital devices with no software installation, configuration or hassle. You can easily:

* Connect dozens of digital cameras with no additional software.

* Connect dozens of displays with no additional software.

* Connect hundreds of printers with no additional software.

* Connect dozens of DV camcorders with no additional software.

* Connect dozens of input devices, including Bluetooth keyboards and mice, game controllers and graphics tablets, with no additional software.

* Connect many scanners without additional software.

* Connect Bluetooth devices such as mobile phones and input devices securely with encryption.

* Connect audio and MIDI devices over USB or FireWire.

* Connect storage devices and optical media with no additional software.

* Print directly to Windows shared printers over the SMB protocol.

* Send faxes using your built-in modem or Bluetooth mobile phone, complete with cover sheet from any application.

* Receive faxes using your built-in modem.

* Answer incoming voice calls on V.92 modems while connected to the Internet.

* Automatically enhance images while scanning with Image Capture.

* Share your USB printer with others in your home, even those on Windows-based machines.

Mac OS X offers built-in support for PC networking services, called SMB. As a result, the Mac is at home on PC networks (or just about any other kind), making the business of sharing files and printers with PCs entirely painless. And in Mac OS X you don't have to be a network administrator to make it all work, just browse your local network from any Finder window. You can network without cables inside your house using AirPort or another wireless access point. Of course, you can also swap files via data CD, floppies or Zip disks. And most new peripherals connect via USB or FireWire, so you can use them with either PCs or Macs.

Some FAQs on OS X

Installing Mac OS X is dead easy, and updates and fixes are always available from the Apple web site. However, despite the apparent simplicity of Mac OS X, there are always the inevitable FAQs. Some of the regularly asked questions are:

Do I need to upgrade all my Mac OS 9 applications to Mac OS X versions?
No, you can run almost any Mac OS 9 application in the Mac OS X Classic environment. This means that you can take full advantage of all the great features of Mac OS X, and at the same time, run your existing applications.

Are there Mac OS X versions of my software?
It depends, but most likely, yes. To date, vendors have

developed more than 6,500 native applications for Mac OS X. Moreover, quite a few of these have no equivalent on Mac OS 9. The critically acclaimed iLife applications – iMovie 3, iTunes 4, iPhoto 2 and iDVD 3 – let you organise and create digital media with elegant simplicity. And with Panther you can make graphically dynamic presentations with Keynote, edit video like a pro with Final Cut Express, keep your calendar and contacts organised with iCal and iSync, or get the fastest Web surfing from Safari.

Are my iTunes and iMovie files convertible?
You can import your projects into iMovie 3 and use your MP3 files with iTunes 4. In addition, you'll find iPhoto 2 to organise your digital pictures. Mac OS X makes it easy to use the iLife applications. When you plug in your digital camera, it launches iPhoto. When you plug in your camcorder, it launches iMovie. When you insert an audio CD, it launches iTunes. How much easier could it get?

Can I use my printer?
Panther comes loaded with many printer drivers so you don't have to install driver software when you upgrade. When you plug in your USB printer, Panther will automatically detect it and load its driver. All you have to do is select the Printer in the Print Centre Application and

you're ready to go. You can also confirm your printer is compatible with Mac OS X.

Can I use my existing hardware devices?
You can use your digital camera, your scanner, your camcorder, and the many other hardware peripherals. There's no need to fear because Panther works with most USB or FireWire peripherals on the market today. And you won't lose any time re-installing any software drivers to use the device because Mac OS X comes loaded with most of the drivers you might need. All you need to do is plug in your peripheral and start using it.

Can my Mac run Mac OS X?
As mentioned in a bit more detail earlier on in this book, in order to run Mac OS X, you'll need at least 128MB of physical RAM and at least 3GB of available space on your hard disk for the installation. And your Mac needs to be one of the models that can run Mac OS X. See the list of compatible Macs.

Do I need a new video card?
Don't be silly...we're talking about a Mac here. The Mac OS X Quartz graphics subsystem delivers crisp graphics, anti-aliased fonts, and blends 2D, 3D and QuickTime content

together with transparency and drop shadows. No other operating system delivers the high-quality graphics rendering of Quartz. However, if you want to let Quartz Extreme accelerate this graphic rendering, you will need a video card with a particular chip (NVIDIA GeForce2 MX, GeForce3, GeForce4 MX or GeForce4 Ti, or any AGP-based ATI RADEON GPU) and a minimum of 16MB VRAM. You can only install these cards in Power Macs.

Is it easy to learn Mac OS X?

Mac OS X is extremely easy to learn and a joy to use. There are plenty of new features to get to know, but they come with a built-in help system that guides you through the process. And of course, Mac OS X continues Apple's traditional leadership in ease-of-use. When you pick up knowledge in one application, you can apply it to other uses. Take a learning tour through Mac OS X.

How easy is it to install Mac OS X?

If you're upgrading from Mac OS 8, 9, or an earlier version of Mac OS X it doesn't take long to install Mac OS X v10.3 'Panther', so don't worry about losing any productivity.

Do I need to know UNIX to run Mac OS X?

Absolutely not, and you'd probably run a mile if you did.

Mac OS X almost alchemically marries the power of UNIX with the simplicity of Macintosh, and that means you don't have to know a thing about how UNIX works, or even what it is, to take advantage of its reliability, security and power. As with Mac OS 9, you can control your computing experience with a mouse, keyboard and graphical interface.

So, basically, Mac OS X is a good idea for just about everything you need to do on your Mac, not just for downloading music. But do try to keep up with system updates and download often. It will go a long way to keeping both you and your Mac happy and stress-free.

Ripping Your Own Music

Everyone has a record or CD collection and if you've acquired an iPod, you'll probably want to include some of that collection on your new toy. Despite the name, with CDs and iTunes, 'ripping' music from a CD is actually a fairly painless process. In simple terms, all it means is that you're converting recordings into digital files on your computer and with the proper iTunes settings, ripping a CD track and preparing it for use with your iPod couldn't be easier.

Before you begin ripping your favourite CD, you need to decide which format you want for your music. All the main music file formats you'll probably need are described earlier in this book. From within iTunes, choose Preferences on the Mac or Edit-Preferences on the PC, click the Importing tab and choose the file format you want from the pop-up menu. When you turn on 'Create files names with track number', songs you're importing are arranged in the same order in iTunes as they are on your CD – even if you leave out certain tracks.

You might get a surprise when you insert your CD into your Mac or PC and discover that the album just gets anonymously named 'Audio CD' and that all the songs are called 'Track 1, Track 2', etc. The reason for this is that most audio CDs just don't include any digital information about anything other than the music files.

However, with iTunes, there's a way round this. After you load your CD you can type in all the song information by:

1   clicking the individual track's name once it's highlighted and then

2   clicking again to open up the renaming box where you can edit to your heart's content.

▲	Song	Time
1	☑ Track 01	3:43
2	☑ Track 02	2:23
3	☑ Track 03	2:47
4	☑ Track 04	3:11
5	☑ Track 05	3:42
6	☑ Track 06	2:35

▲	Song	Time
1	☑ Track 01	3:43
2	☑ Track 02	2:23
3	☑ Track 03	2:47
4	☑ Track 04	3:11
5	☑ Track 05	3:42
6	☑ Track 06	2:35

▲	Song	Time
1	☑ Track 01	3:43
2	☑ Track 02	2:23
3	☑ Track 03	2:47
4	☑ santa monica	3:11
5	☑ Track 05	3:42
6	☑ Track 06	2:35

Once you're happy with your naming process and you've included all the other details you feel you'll need, each song will have a checkbox next to its name which indicates that iTunes will convert and copy it to your computer when you click the Import button. If there's anything on a particular album you don't want, simply un-check the box before you click the Import button in the upper right-hand corner of the screen. When you've finished importing, each song will have a green check-mark and, voila – you'll have another set of new files in your iTunes Library.

The Next Step: GarageBand

Although CDs and the iTune Store may be your main source of music, it's good to remember that not all sound files come directly from these sort of sources. A nice feature of iTunes is that as long as a file is in a format that it can understand, you can add music to your library from a variety of sources – including those you create yourself. There are a number of digital sequencers, or 'recording studios in your computer', which allow you to record, edit, augment and mix, just as you would in a professional recording studio. Market favourites such as CuBase or ProTools are all interesting, depending on the seriousness of your approach.

But Apple has also entered the fray with its own 'studio in a box' in the guise of an application called GarageBand.

GarageBand turns your Mac into an anytime, anywhere recording studio packed with hundreds of instruments and a recording engineer or two for good measure. It's the easiest way yet to create, perform and record your own music whether you're an accomplished player or just a tacky Pop Idol wannabe. And, GarageBand is the newest member of the iLife family, so you can use it to easily add your original music to your slideshows, DVD menus, burn it to CDs or score iMovie projects.

GarageBand claims that you don't have to play the piano, you don't have to read music, and, you don't even have to have rhythm. I would probably take issue with that if you're at all serious about music, but there is no disputing the fact that if you know what you like when you hear it, you can make your own kind of music with GarageBand. And, it probably is the easiest way for anyone, pro or novice alike, to perform, record and create music.

GarageBand features
GarageBand turns your Mac into a digital recording studio – complete with instruments, pre-recorded loops,

amps, effects and editing tools. Apple has even seen fit to include an assortment of virtual recording engineers in the mix to help you out. But, how easy is it to create your own music in GarageBand? If you know how to click and drag and drop, you're well on your way to becoming a GarageBand adept.

Since not everyone has a garage, let alone a band to invite over, Apple thought we might appreciate having a few professional musicians sit in on our sessions. That's why you'll find more than a thousand of their riffs on your Mac after you install GarageBand. These are basically professionally-recorded Apple Loops and are all royalty-free interludes, played in a variety of moods and genres, on many different instruments. These Loops form the building blocks for your songs and you can place them in infinite combinations of unique arrangements. Need a longer sound? Loops extend to any length you want. You can adjust the volume and balance of each track individually, even fade the volume of a selected track in or out.

If you are musically inclined, you can do even more with GarageBand. You can, for instance, plug your guitar, keyboard or microphone into your Mac to record your own parts and lean on GarageBand to supply all the backing tracks you need. Just pick and choose what you like to set the foundation or backing tracks, then lay down a few tracks of your own to complete the mix. If you happen to be a guitar player, you also have access to virtual guitar amps that let you emulate such classic and modern sounds with names like Clean Jazz, Arena Rock and others.

Once you're satisfied with your mix you can export to iTunes for instant access from your iTunes Music Library. In fact, iTunes4.2 automatically creates a playlist in your name – which is nearly as good as 15 minutes of fame. From there you can burn it to a CD, transfer it to your iPod or use it in one of your iPhoto, iMovie or iDVD projects, just like any other song in iTunes.

System requirements

GarageBand is now part of the iLife suite and details and pricing is readily available on the Apple web site. Keep in mind the fact that you'll need at least the following systems/configurations to use GarageBand.

- Macintosh computer with a PowerPC G3, G4 or G5 processor

- 600MHz G3 or faster required for GarageBand

- G4 or faster required for GarageBand software instruments

- 733MHz G4 or faster required for iDVD

- 256MB of physical RAM

- Mac OS X v10.2.6 or later (Mac OS X v10.2.8 or later recommended)

- QuickTime 6.4 or later (QuickTime 6.5 included)

- Display with at least 1024-by-768-pixel resolution

- DVD drive required to install GarageBand and iDVD

- 4.3GB of disk space required to install all iLife applications; or 250MB to install iTunes, iPhoto and iMovie only.

Using you Mac or PC as a proper recording studio can be a fascinating and creative experience and there are a number of software applications that would probably suit any musician's needs. It's a subject that's just a bit too big for a book like this. (However, if you do want to find out more about this sort of thing, check out the other books available on the Sanctuary list.)

Part Three - Other Stuff

Glossary of Downloading Terms

A

AAC: Advanced Audio Coding. Designed to replace MP3 technology, which is more than a decade old, this sound compression system is far more efficient and delivers better sound quality, rivalling that of uncompressed CDs. Even modem users will hear the difference. This is the compression technology used by the latest version of Apple's iPod portable music player.

access time: the amount of time required for a drive to locate and retrieve a piece of information, as measured in milliseconds. A drive with a low access time yields the best recording quality.

acoustic: musical instruments that are not electronically amplified.

adapter: a physical connector that bridges two differing types of input and output ports.

ADC: analog-to-digital converter. The device used for recording and converting sound into numbers. See digitize.

AIFF: Audio Interchange File Format. The Macintosh format for the storage of digital sound.

airplay: the broadcast of a recording or music video on radio or television.

album: a collection of individual musical works conceived and manufactured as a unit; the physical media may be CD, cassette tape, or vinyl LP. See track.

analog: recorded sound that has not been converted to

numbers; a recording and playback method where the speed and loudness of sound waves is reflected in a similar fashion onto a CD or magnetic tape. See digitize.

Analog: a logfile analyzer program that tracks usage patterns on a web server. Some information Analog captures is the frequency an individual page is visited, the country a user is from, and the link they followed to arrive at the site.

ASFS: an encoded compressed music file format used by Virtuosa Gold.

AudibleManager: software that allows you to manage your audio content; used to download audio files directly to your computer, transfer them to your portable audio player, burn them to a CD, and listen to them on your PC.

audio file: music or sounds that are collected under a single heading and digitized and compressed for storage, or for transfer to a player system.

Audio Home Recording Act: A 1992 US law that, among other things, gave increased freedom to copy music for personal, home use.

audiophile: an enthusiast of high-quality sound.

auxiliary: a socket on a sound card enabling the connection of additional audio playing equipment. See jack.

B

bit: the smallest unit of measure of data storage capacity. See byte; RAM.

bit rate: the quantity of storage space used by a piece of music or data, as measured in kilobits per second. See Kbps.

bootleg: illegally recorded, manufactured, traded or sold copyrighted music. Also known as piracy.

bootlegger: a person or group that illegally records or trades copyrighted music. Also known as a pirate

broadcast: the electronic transmission of sound or image through waves that can be reconstituted by a receiver mechanism.
bug: an error in a computer program that causes it to malfunction.

burn: to write information onto a CD-R or CD-RW disc.

burner: a device that writes information onto a CD-R or CD-RW disc.

BURN-proof: buffer under-run proof. A program that seamlessly reconnects any gaps that occur when burning a disc, due to interruption of the data system.

byte: a measure of data storage capacity equal to 8 bits, which is the standard length of alphanumeric identification codes.

C

cardioid microphone: a microphone designed to capture sound created directly in front of it, while disregarding background noise. See omnidirectional microphone.

catalogue: 1) A directory of files or recordings stored on a disc. 2) The list of copyrights owned by a music publisher, or recording masters owned by a record company.

CBR: constant bit rate. An MP3 file compressing each second of recorded sound to the same size. See VBR.

CDA: compact disc audio. The encoding method used to store uncompressed sound on a standard CD.

CD-DA: compact disc digital audio. An early standard for recording sound on CD. See Red Book.

CDDB: compact disc database. An online index of CD album information.

CD-quality sound: a term for sound recorded at 16 bits, the standard rate for recording music on CD.

CD-R: compact disc-recordable. 1) A CD that can be written onto in a single work session, read from multiple times, but cannot be added to at a later work session, erased, or reused. 2) The media typically used to burn CD-ROMs and audio CDs on a home computer. See WORM disc; CD-RW.

CD-ROM: compact disc read-only memory. The full name for a data storage CD.

CD-RW: compact disc rewriteable. A CD that can be added to over multiple work sessions, or erased and reused. Most CD-RW drives are able to use both CD-R and CD-RW discs, but not all CD-R drives can use CD-RW discs.

channel: refers to the process of getting digital music into the marketplace. Includes the artist, record label, distributor, retailer, consumer, and anyone else providing technology or services along the way.

chart: industry ranking of recordings according to rate of sales and/or broadcast.

check-in: the process or ability to return a music file from a portable player to a hard drive.

check-out: the process or ability to transfer a music file from a hard drive to a portable player.

clearance: permission granted to reproduce a copyrightable work.

clipboard: a temporary holding place in RAM for information copied or cut.

codec: compression/decompression. Any hardware or software system for digitizing and condensing audio or video data into a smaller number of bits for storage or transmission, and for restoring that data to its original size and format for replay. See compress; decompress; digitize.

compress: an efficient coding of data that reduces the amount of memory space required for storage, or time to transfer it. Compressed data must be decompressed before it is available for use.

condenser microphone: a battery-powered microphone designed to capture low volume nuances of sound, such as a whisper.

configuration: the media format on which a recording is fixed, such as cassette, CD or DVD.

converter: a software function that converts one file format to another.

copyright: the legal right of ownership and control over artistic or intellectual property, such as a book, game, image, movie, music, software, video, or website, controlling its use, distribution and reproduction. For more information about international copyright registration, visit www.copyrightwitness.com or www.copysite.com.

counterfeit recording: a 'pirate' recording that is duplicated and sold with the intent to defraud the legitimate owner of royalties.

cover: a performance of a song by an artist other than the one who originally recorded it.

crossover: when a recording gains sales or is broadcast in more than a single market format.

crosstalk: the leaking of sound from one track to another on audiotape.

D

DAC: digital-to-analog converter. A sound card enabling digital audio sound files to be replayed.

DAE: digital audio extraction. The system used by a CD-ROM drive to transfer digital audio data from an audio CD to a computer.

data: information a computer needs in order to make decisions or carry out a particular action.

DAM CD: digital automatic music compact disc. The media used by MP3.com to burn both MP3 and standard audio CD formatted music onto the same disc. This allows the disc to be played on a home CD player, or copied to a hard drive MP3 file or into an MP3 player.

data: 1) Information a computer needs in order to make a decision or execute a particular action.
2) Information stored in RAM for future access.

data buffer: a system of temporary storage, enabling the

smooth transfer of streaming audio information without breaking up.

daughterboard: a small card that plugs into a sound card to give it additional capabilities.

decibel: the unit of measure of the volume of sound.

decode: to return an encoded audio file to un-encoded and uncompressed digital audio data.

decompress: to return compressed data to its original form prior to using it. Compression provides efficient storage or transfer of data.

demo: demonstration recording of a song or performance.

digital: a recording system where images, sounds or text are captured and converted by computer into a high-speed binary pulse code of number patterns, for storage on magnetic tape, compact disc, CD, DVD or hard drive.

digital audio: sound recorded as a series of numbers.

digital sampling: sound transformed and stored as a

numerical sequence, which can then be reproduced in such a way as to be indistinguishable from the original sound.

digital wallet: software used by online retailers to encrypt and retain consumer information such as identification, credit card number, and shipping information.

digitize: the conversion of analog audio into digital audio. Analog sound waves are broken down into consecutive miniscule increments, measured, and converted into a complex series of numbers that replicates the volume and quality of the original sound pattern.

distortion: 1) The 'bending' of sound to create new effects, 2) Unwanted noise.

distributor: a person or company that supplies recorded products to retailers.

docking station: the connection point between a portable MP3 player and a PC, for transferring audio data from computer files to the MP3 player.

download: the transfer of a file or program from one computer to another, generally from a larger host system or server to a smaller client system, through a modem or network connection. See upload.

DSP: digital signal processor. A computer system for adding effects such as echo or reverb to sound.

dubbing: improving the quality of recorded sound by inserting new pieces of audio to correct imperfections.
dynamic microphone: a microphone designed to capture high volume sound.

E

edit: to modify parameters or alter existing data.

encode: 1) to convert data into a particular file format, such as converting a WAV file to an MP3 file; 2) To encrypt (convert data into code to prevent unauthorised use).

encryption: any procedure used to convert data files to mathematical code so that unauthorised recipients cannot read the data. An encrypted file cannot be accessed without using an assigned password to unlock the code.

end user: an individual that employs hardware or software created by another.

equalization: the manipulation of recorded audio frequencies to improve sound quality.

error message: a communication from a program alerting its user that an inaccuracy of some type has occurred.

F

fair use: the legal guideline for reproducing copyrighted material without a licence.

file: data or information that is grouped together under a single heading, digitally converted to bytes, and stored in a portion of a software program.

file extension: the 3-letter code after the full stop on an audio file name, indicating the codec used on that file. See codec.

filter: the removal of pops, hiss, or ambient noise from a recording.

flash memory: a computer system that prevents data loss when electrical power fails.

floppy disc: a portable storage unit for digital information.

freeware: computer programs available without charge to the general public.

frequency: the vibrating pattern of a sound wave that

determines pitch.

fulfillment: industry term which, at its simplest, means that the audio file consumer is provided with whatever digital data or plug-in is necessary to play the music as it was intended.

FTP: file transfer protocol. A system for online file transfer.

G

General MIDI: a numbering system used in recording that assigns an order to electronic instrument sounds, beginning with piano and ending with special sound effects. See MIDI.

gigabyte: a unit of storage capacity equal to 1 billion bytes.

Gold: the RIAA designation for records that sell 500,000 wholesale copies or videos that sell 50,000 wholesale copies. See platinum.

H

hard drive: a computer's data storage hardware, whose memory capacity is expressed in megabytes.

hardware: tangible pieces of computer equipment.

High Sierra: a format for use on CD-ROM that allows files and directories to be read by DOS.

I

ID3 Tag: the space on a sound file for adding textual information about the recording.

iMix: user-created playlists, often including liner notes, available for downloading through iTunes Music Store.

independent artist: a recording artist that is not under contract to a major record company.

independent distributor: a wholesaler of a product from independent record labels.

independent label: a record label not affiliated with any of the major recorded music conglomerates.

indie: short for 'independent.'

infringement: the act of violating the rights of a copyright owner.

internal flash: a MP3 player's flash memory storage.

interoperability: the ability of computer hardware and software components to work together and share resources.

iPod: manufactured by Apple, it is the most popular brand of digital music player. Ultra portable, an iPod weighs less than a couple of CDs and can fit into your pocket. Some models can hold up to 10,000 songs, thousands of digital photos, games, and serve as a personal voice recorder. Models are available for Macintosh and Windows users.

ISO: International Standards Organization. Sets standards for engineering and design concerns.

ISO-9660: the predecessor of High Sierra.

ISRC: International Standard Recording Code. The unique alphanumeric identifier assigned to each recording and encoded into every copy of that recording for the tracking of royalty payments.

iTunes Music Store: Apple Computer's online music store sells tracks for downloading, creates cover art for jewel cases, and offers a range of additional services.

J

jack: the point of connection, or socket, where two pieces of equipment are joined by a cable.

jewel case: the plastic case enclosing a CD.

jingle: a short song used in radio and television product advertising.

jitter correction: a program feature that removes distortion occurring during digital audio extraction (ripping), or when digitized audio files are converted to analog.

jukebox: refers to the software or the actual equipment that organises and plays digital music files.

K

Kbps: kilobits per second. A measurement of audio data storage space used by a piece of music per second of its downloading. See bit rate; kilobit.

kilobit: a measurement equal to 1,024 bits.

L

label: an individual record company, or one of several product names under which a record company releases its recordings.

LCD: liquid crystal display. The text information viewing screen seen on MP3 players, audio equipment, and cell phones.

leech: slang term for a person who downloads quantities of MP3 files without posting any in return.

licence: the terms under which permission granted for a copyrighted work to be used.

licence agreement: the acceptance of the user of a copyrighted work to obey the terms of use spelled out in the licence.

line in: a socket on a sound card enabling the connection of other audio playing equipment. See auxiliary.

long form: a music video that is longer than five minutes or is made up of several songs.

lossless: 1) Any compression method resulting in a decompressed file that is not identical to the original uncompressed file; 2) Any reproduction method where the copy is an exact replica of the original.

lossy compression: 1) Any compression method resulting in a decompressed file that is identical to the original uncompressed file; 2) Any reproduction method where the copy is not an exact replica of the original.

M

major label: one of the conglomerate music recording companies owning its own distribution system.

master: the final, multi-track mix of a recording, either on tape or cut into a lacquer master disc, from which copies will be manufactured.

mechanical licence: permission granted by the owner of a copyrighted song for a new recording of that song to be made.

media: the physical instrument onto which data, images or music is encoded, ie: film, audio tape, floppy disc, CD, etc.

megabyte: a measure of data storage capacity equal to one million bytes.

memory: data storage capacity, as expressed in megabytes. See RAM.

memory card: a new and expensive technology that allows up to 64 Mbs of data to be stored on a small, portable card.

merchandising: any product that utilises an artist's image, name, or likeness to promote that artist.

mic in: a socket on a sound card enabling the connection of a microphone.

microdrive: a very small hard drive that can substitute for a flash memory.

middleware: software that enables two or more independent programs or systems to communicate. See XML.

MIDI. musical instrument digital interface. In effect, it is the digital equivalent of sheet music. A system for storing music as a series of computer files that instruct electronic instruments on which notes to play, and when. See General MIDI.

miniplug: the kind of plug typically used to connect headphones to portable music players.

mix/final mix: the combination of multiple audio tracks into one or two tracks/the combination of multiple audio tracks into the final, two-track tape from which a master will be made.

MP3: common usage of the name MPEG-1 Audio Layer 3. A system for compressing audio data files to nearly one-tenth their original size, while maintaining CD-quality sound. Roughly, one minute of audio data = 1 MB of space at 128 Kbps.

MP3pro: an audio codec designed by Thompson Multimedia to offer MP3-quality sound in smaller compressed files.

MP4: the catchall term for systems, such as AAC, that improve upon the decade-old MP3 technology. Improvements include streaming over the Internet, variable frame and bit rates, and the addition of subtitles and pictures.

MPEG: Moving Picture Expert Group. An ISO sub-committee that sets official standards relating to digitized audio and video technology.

MPMan: a popular brand of MP3 players manufactured by Saehan.

multisession CD-R: a CD-R drive that allows data to be added to a disc during different sessions.

multi-voice: the ability to electronically reproduce the sounds of more than one instrument simultaneously.

MusicMatch Jukebox: a Microsoft Windows program for creating and playing digital audio formats such as CD, MP3, and WAV. The program also includes music management features that display cover art, lyrics, track notes, and artist bios for each track as it plays, allow tracks to be sorted by artist, title, category, etc, and create automated playlists.

N

Napster: the 1999 brainchild of then-teenager Shawn Fanning, this ground-breaking music downloading mega-site once operated outside of copyright regulations. Napster now offers legal access to hundreds of thousands of tracks for a minimal monthly fee.

newsgroup: a large group of Internet discussion areas formed around a specific topic.

normalizing: adjusting audio files to a consistent volume level.

O

omnidirectional microphone: a microphone designed to capture sound from all directions, not just those immediately in front of it.

Orange Book: the industry standard for WORM discs used to back up text files. See WORM disc.

P

Party Shuffle: a playlist feature offered by iTunes Music Store that automatically sorts, selects and plays random tracks from a user's collection in much the same way that a DJ would.

patch: a small computer program used to modify or update another program.

peer-to-peer distribution: the unauthorised trade or distribution of copyrighted material between consumers. The exchange of information about a product does not infringe on copyright law.

persistent access: a legal term meaning that a consumer has the right to listen to legally acquired music whenever he wishes.

persistent protection: a legal term meaning that copyright protection remains in force at all times and in all places.

PII: personally identifiable information. Industry jargon for any electronic identification data that can be tied to a specific human being.

piracy: the unauthorised duplication and sale of sound recordings.

phono cable: cable used primarily to connect audio equipment and sound cards.

platinum: the RIAA designation for records that sell 1,000,000 wholesale copies or videos that sell 100,000 wholesale copies.

player: the equipment or program that decodes and replays digital audio files.

playlist: a menu of song titles to select from for replay. Jukebox software can tag tracks with cover art, lyrics and notes, sort tracks by artist, title, and category, or create automatic playlists based upon user-established sorting preferences.

plug: the connection device, usually on the end of a cable, that is inserted into a socket to connect audio equipment together.

plug-in: a program file that enhances the functions of a larger program.

PnP: plug and play. The ability of a computer to automatically recognise and configure a new piece of add-on hardware without the need to physically configure the hardware with jumpers or switches.

portable media: any type of media that can be transferred between players.

public domain: lapsed or never-copyrighted material that is available free of charge for general public use.

QuickTime: a program able to read most non-proprietary audio or video formats, including streaming Internet and virtual reality movies.

R

RAM: stands for 'random access memory'. The data storage capacity of a hard drive, measured in bytes. See byte.

RCA audio cable: typically used to connect home stereo systems, the cable's plug uses a metal 'sleeve' that slides over a round metal aperture.

RealAudio: a popular sound format typically used for Internet streaming, of inferior sound quality to MP3.

realtime: when a live performance is viewed on a monitor at virtually the same time as it is broadcast.

Red Book: the industry standard for CD Digital Audio, referring to a CD that contains recorded music without additional computer programs.

release: a recording available to the public for purchase.

release date: the actual day a recording is first available to the public for purchase.

reverb: an electronically produced echo effect with a depth of sound.

RIAA: Recording Industry Association of America. A trade group formed to administer the interests of the recording industry, especially the tracking of sales figures.

Rio: a popular personal MP3 player manufactured by Diamond Multimedia.

rip: to transfer digital audio data from an audio CD to a hard drive.

ripper: software that transfers digital audio data from an audio CD to a hard drive.

rotation: the number of times a given song is played during the course of a radio station's daily or weekly playlist.

royalty: a fee paid to the owner of a copyright or patent for the right to use the intellectual property.

S

sample: 1) The single digital measurement of a sound wave at any given point. A series of consecutive samples is made to digitize an entire song; 2) Brief segments of existing recorded sounds or songs that are incorporated into a new work.

sampling rates: the frequency with which a computer samples an audio recording as it digitizes it for file storage. The higher the sampling rate, the better the sound quality, and the bigger the file.

SanDisc: a system of flash memory. See flash memory.

scan: to mechanically transform a document or image into electronic digital data which can be stored in a computer file.

scanner: a sort of digital copy machine that 'prints' a copy of a document or image into a computer memory file.

SCSI: small computer system interface. A format for linking up computer hardware.

SCSI port: the device included on a special SCSI card required to link up some CD-ROM drives.

SCSI/2: the new and improved SCSI.

SDMI: secure digital music initiative. A digital audio file format created with the intent of alleviating recording industry concerns over copyright protection.

search engine: a website clearinghouse of information about other websites, collected for viewing in response to user request.

skin: a file that offers alternative visual covers (skins) for a program without affecting its operation.

shareware: an honour system whereby a publisher allows a consumer to try out software free of charge for a specific period of time before committing to buy it.

short form: a music video containing a single song.

SHOUTcast: a popular Internet radio station website found at www.shoutcast.com.

signal: the electronic pattern representing sound waves.

SmartMedia: a popular brand of flash memory cards used by various personal digital devices like MP3 players.

socket: see jack.

software: the intangible programs and information used by a computer to enable various functions. See hardware.

Sonique: a brand of software that plays digital audio files like MP3.

sound card: the internal computer device that converts digital audio file data into sound for speakers, and digitizes external sound for transfer to audio data files.

sound file: See audio file.

SoundBlaster-compatible: a sound card that operates with any software written for the SoundBlaster card.

sound recording: a recorded audio performance that is captured in a tangible medium, considered an artistic work, and qualifies for copyright protection.

soundtrack: 1) the audio portion of a film;
2) a record album containing the musical portions of a film.

streaming audio: sound that is digitized, sent over the Internet, reconverted to analog, received, and played at virtually the same time as it is originally broadcast. Digital radio stations operate in this manner.

superdistribution: industry term for the authorised distribution of a product between consumers, sometimes with an incentive provided to the initiating party.

synthesised: musical sounds and sound effects artificially created by computer hardware.

The Art of Downloading Music

T

tag: a brief descriptive label embedded into text to identify individual elements.

terabyte: a measure of data storage capacity equal to one trillion bytes.

tethered system: an MP3 player designed to remain connected to a PC.

theme: same as skin.

time out: a music track promotionally available for a limited time is said to have timed out when the promotional period expires.

track: a single work of recorded music, regardless of length. Can be combined with other tracks to form an album.

transfer: 1) Any of a variety of connection systems between a computer and an MP3 player; 2) The act of transmitting data, such as a file or program, from one location to another.

tray-loading: a CD-ROM drive featuring a drawer-like tray that slides open to accept a CD.

tweaking: manually fine-tuning an audio or video recording to achieve the best sound or picture quality.

upload: the process of transferring a file or program from one computer to another, generally from a smaller client system to a larger host system or server, through a modem or network connection. See download.

user: any device, individual or group of people that employs software or hardware to perform a task. See end user.

V

VBR: variable bit rate. A format that digitally encodes sounds at a variable rate, using a heightened sampling rate (thus more storage space) for complex passages, and a much lower rate for pauses.

video: an electronic medium combining audio and visual elements that is stored on videotape or videodisc, broadcast via airwaves, and viewed on a television or a monitor.

video jockey: a television announcer/host who plays music videos as part of his show.

viral marketing: industry term for the peer-to-peer promotion and/or distribution of information about a product, rather than the exchange of the actual product itself.

Virtuosa Gold: a brand of program that encodes and plays digital audio files for MP3s.

VJ: see video jockey.

VQF: Vector Quantization Format. A freebie codec that claims to be superior to MP3, but works the computer harder and is not MP3 compatible.

voice: a term for an individual synthesised musical instrument sound.

W

watermark: a pattern embedded into a digital music file to identify copyright information, and which is designed to survive any form of copying or transmission.

WAV: a format for transferring sound to uncompressed digital audio files. This produces the best sound quality.

Webcasting: Internet radio stations that typically play MP3s through computer servers.

Winamp: a popular brand of MP3 player program that offers many extra features.

Windows CE: a miniaturised version of Microsoft Windows that operates on pocket PCs and can play MP3s.

WMA: Windows Media Audio. This Microsoft answer to MP3 compresses audio files one quarter smaller than an MP3, without sacrificing sound quality.

WORM disc: acronym for write once, read many. CD media that can be written to once and read multiple times, but cannot be erased and reused. See CD-R.

XML: a standard electronic language used in creating tags that can be read by many different systems and programs. See tag.

Yellow Book: the industry standard for CDs containing computer programs and information.

MP3 and Music Related Websites

Where to find MP3s

www.apple.com/itunes/download

At the iTunes Music Store you can purchase albums or single tracks, browse Billboard charts, view music videos, search for audio books, and burn CDs.

www.napster.com

Napster has returned – all legal and with over 750,000 tracks and growing. New releases are added every Tuesday. Download MP3s or listen online to over 50 interactive commercial-free radio stations. The first 7 days are free, then a monthly fee is charged to remain a subscriber.

www.musicmatch.com

Winner of *PC Magazine* Editor's Choice award for Best Music Player five times in a row, MusicMatch's site has a jukebox, radio, and music store with downloads for a small fee. The site can be accessed in Dutch, English, French, Italian, Portuguese, and Spanish.

www.emusic.com

The first 50 MP3 downloads from the catalogue of over 400,000 songs are free at emusic, but to continue service, a low monthly fee is assessed. Mix and burn your own CDs at no extra charge.

http://musarchive.com

For a small monthly fee, MusicArchive subscribers receive unlimited access to the music and movies catalogue of downloads. Search by artist, album or song title.

www.real.com/rhapsody

Rhapsody charges a small fee to burn your own CD from a catalogue of over 600,000 songs. Videos, free games and over 60 ad-free radio stations.

The Art of Downloading Music

http://mp3.sound-maniac.com
A monthly subscription fee gives subscribers unlimited downloads of MP3s and movies. Search by title or genre: alternative, blues, classics, dance, disco, electronic, folk, gospel, hip-hop, pop, R&B, rock, romances, singer/songwriter.

www.mp3downloadhq.com
MP3 Download Headquarters claims to have unlimited downloads of music and movies for free, but there is a nominal monthly fee assessed.

www.freecds.com
At freeCDs.com you have to open an account and then earn points by participating in various offers, such as applying for a credit card or joining eBay, that can then be exchanged for 'free' CDs or an MP3 player.

Other Popular MP3 Sites

www.buymusic.com

In the catalogue of nearly half a million songs and growing, you will find every genre of music represented, from alternative to oldies, metal to new age, hip-hop to soundtracks, to purchase MP3s from. Part of buy.com, where you can find deals on books, cameras, electronics, games, music, and toys – check out the 'Today's Deals' tab.

www.cnet.com

If you can't find the technology information you need in CNET's massive directory, it probably doesn't exist. Find tech news, product reviews and price comparisons, for everything from desktop and notebook computers to handhelds, cell phones, drivers and burners, home audio and video, Internet services, peripherals, and of course, MP3 and digital music. Click on the 'downloads' tab for music, games and software.

www.dailymp3.com

As you might have guessed from the name, DailyMP3 posts new information about nearly everything you would want to know about MP3 software, hardware and related news every day. Search, read about and download from the massive directory of burners, converters, encoders, games, playlist makers, plugins, rippers, screensavers and skins. Visit daily for the latest and greatest.

www.listen.com

Since 1998, San Francisco-based Listen.com has been building one of the largest and most comprehensive directories of where to find legitimately posted music on the Web by mega artists, as well as up-and-comers. In 2001, Listen launched Rhapsody, which quickly became one of the largest digital music subscription services. Burn CDs, download MP3s, or listen to music from the site's radio station.

www.mp3.com

Before most noticed the budding enthusiasm of downloadable music, MP3.com snagged rights to the name and began amassing one of the largest archives of legally traded MP3s on the Web. The extensive catalogue can be searched by artist, album or genre, including bluegrass, blues, children's, country, electronic-dance, folk, gospel-spiritual, hip-hop, jazz, Latin, new age, radio/books/spoken, rock/pop, R&B/soul/urban, vocal-easy listening, and world/reggae. The site also has thousands of free downloads from independent artists.

Sites that Rank other Sites

www.top25mp3.com

Updated every 15 minutes and reset each night, Top25MPs ranks MP3 sites on a Top 25 list with brief descriptions. A 'surfer friendly' icon is awarded to high quality sites. There is also a 'Site of the Moment' recommended and a link to rankings 26-50.

www.wide-gate.com/index.php?usr=top25mp3

Touted as 'The Best MP3 Resources on the Internet', wide-gate has a short list of 12 sites, short narrative, and a keyword search engine that links you to MP3Search.ru for albums and songs.

http://sound-maniac.com

Sound Maniac features 8 sites with current and previous rankings, and descriptions, and a full album search engine that links to another site where you can purchase MP3 downloads.

Online Music Magazines

www.artistdirect.com

Bursting onto the Internet in 1994, Artistdirect is the place to find everything you ever wanted to know about every artist in the world. Search by artist, genre or year, the site has news, charts, concert info, radio stations, musician resources, merchandise, videos and much more. Download an entire album or purchase tickets for featured concerts.

www.dotmusic.com

Find singles and album charts from Italy, Germany, UK and Spain at dotmusic.com. The UK-based online music magazine is also packed with artist spotlights, music news, radio stations, reviews, videos, and links to purchase CDs and MP3s.

www.mtv.com

Although much of the site is dedicated to information about MTV series and specials, the music area has charts, tour schedules, photos, music news, videos to watch, message boards, and downloads in indie, hip-hop, pop, rock, and soul/R&B genres.

www.noizyland.com

NoiZyland covers the New Zealand indie rock and pop

music scene, with an increasing amount of electronic and dance music being added.

www.pollstar.com

Because it receives weekly updates directly from the artists' booking agents, Pollstar is the best place on the Web to find accurate tour information. You will also find news, classified ads where concert tickets are sometimes offered and show reviews.

www.q4music.com

No, there is not a line to stand in at q4music.com, the online version of Q magazine. Purchase tickets to UK concerts and events, read up on latest music news, listen to Q Radio, join the virtual posse to receive a weekly newsletter and promotions, watch Q TV, and lots of other fun stuff.

www.rollingstone.com

The online version of Rolling Stone has all the features you look for in the magazine: album, concert, and movie reviews, photos, music news and political rants. What the magazine cannot do, that the site does, is feature videos, host RS Radio where you can tune into your favourite streaming music, and sell mainstream MP3 releases.

www.vh1.com/news/newswire/
VH1.com delivers one-stop-shopping for music features, news, and reviews from around the globe, from sources that include BBC Radio 1, Billboard.com, CMT.com, Jam! Showbiz, MTV.com, New Musical Express, Soundgenerator.com, Undercover, and Virginmega.com. Search by artist, source, news, reviews or features; browse photos, find tour dates and charts.

www.vivamusic.com
Vivamusic.com bills itself as 'Asia's leading Music Lifestyle Network'. It covers all genres of music, from rap to classical, dance to R&B, jazz to country, on an easy to search and navigate site, where you'll find the usual features, music news, videos, contests, shopping, Viva Radio, charts and forums.

Hardware, Software and Technical Support

www.apple.com/support/itunes/windows
iPod tutorials, articles and helpful hints for Windows users.

www.dailymp3.com
See description under Most Popular Sites.

www.everythingipod.com
Like the name promises, everthingiPod sells iPods and hundreds of accessories, from cases and clips, to headphones and speakers.

www.ipodhead.com
A place for iPod users to find and exchange information, read the latest news, reviews, rumors and tips.

www.ipodlounge.com
iPodlounge leapt onto the Web just days after the debut of the iPod in late 2001, and has become a leader in providing the latest information about digital audio players, accessories, and related software with articles, reviews, photos of new products, a help area, forum and software downloads.

www.info.apple.com/support/applecore_products/service/ipod_service.html

Apple's webpage for iPod service and support.

www.info.apple.com/usen/ipodwin.
Apple's iPod for Windows technical support with answers to frequently asked questions.

www.ipodebook.com
An ebook packed with tips for getting the maximum use out of your iPod.

www.rioport.com
Originally created to support Diamond's Rio portable MP3 players, the site has software downloads and provides answers to frequently asked questions.

www.mp3.box.sk
An MP3 resource from the Slovak Republic that has music news, hardware and software information, a forum, and links to sites where you can get downloads.

Further Reading

Alderman, John, *Sonic Boom: Napster, MP3 and the New Pioneers of Music*. Boulder, CO: Perseus Book Group, 2001.

Biersdorfer, J.D., *iPod & iTunes: Missing Manual, 2nd Edition*. New York, NY: Pogue Press, 2004.

Bove, Tony and Cheryl Rhodes, *iPod & iTunes for Dummies*. New York, NY: For Dummies, 2003.

Breen, Christopher, *Secrets of the iPod, 4th Edition*. Upper Saddle River, NJ: Pearson Education, 2004.

Briozzo, Gustavo, *MP3 Manual de Referencia*. Chicago, IL: Independent Publishers Group, 2002.

Brown, Roger, *The Complete Idiot's Guide to Music on the Internet with MP3 (The Complete Idiot's Guide)*. Upper Saddle River, NJ: Pearson Professional Education, 2000.

Casale, Fernando and MP Ediciones, *MP3, Volumen II*. CITY: M. P. Ediciones, 2000.

Cohen, Dennis R. and Bob LeVitus, *iTunes, iPhoto, iMovie, and iDVD Bible*. Stafford BC, AUS: John Wiley & Sons, 2003.

Coleman, Mark, *Playback: From the Victrola to MP3, 100 Years of Music, Machines, and Money*. Cambridge, NY: Da Capo Press, 2004.

Dumont, Laura and Jean-Marc Dumont, *MP3: La musique sur Internet*. Nantes Cedex, FRA: ENI, 2003.

Frankel, John, Dave Greely and Ben Sawyer, *MP3 Power! with WinAmp*. Toronto, ONT: Music Sales Corporation, 1999.

Freeman, Brian, *Buzz Your MP3*. New York, NY: Pigeonhole Press, 2001.

Fries, Bruce and Marty Fries, *The Mp3 and Internet Audio Handbook: Your Guide to the Digital Music Revolution*. Burtonsville, MD: Teamcom Books, 2000.

Galvan, Barbara Price, *WebMusic.Com: Making CDs and MP3 Music Free*. Bartlesville, OK: Barbara Price-The Price Company, 1999.

Gortler, Nat and Rod Underhill, *MP3: Musica en Internet Facil*. Upper Saddle River, NJ: Prentice Hall PTR, 2001.

Gilbey, Chris, *MP3 and the Infinite Digital Jukebox: A Step-by-Step Guide to Accessing and Downloading CD Quality Music from the Internet*. St. Paul, MN: Seven Stories Press, 2000.

Hacker, Scott and Simon Hayes, *MP3: The Definitive Guide*. Sebastopol, CA: O'Reilly & Associates, Inc., 2000.

Haring, Bruce and Chuck D., *Beyond the Charts: MP3 and the Digital Music Revolution*. Hollywood, CA: Jm Northern Media, 2000.

Hart-Davis, Guy, *How to Do Everything With Your iPod*. Emeryville, CA: Osborne/McGraw-Hill, 2003.

Hart-Davis, Guy, *MP3 Complete*. London, UK: Sybex Inc., 2000.

Hart-Davis, Guy, *MP3: I didn't Know You Could Do That...*. London, UK: Sybex Inc., 1999.

Hedtke, John and John V. Hedtke, *MP3 and the Digital Music Revolution: Turn Your PC into a CD-Quality Digital Jukebox!* Denver, CO: Top Floor Publishing, 1999.

Hedtke, John V. and Sandy Bradley, *MP3 for Musicians: Promote Your Music Career Online*. Denver, CO: Top Floor Publishing, 2000.

Jamsa, Kris A. and Russell Shaw, *Kris Jamsa's Starting with MP3: Streaming Audio, Video, Multimedia, and Other Cutting-Edge Software*. Quakertown,

PA: Premier Press, 2001.

Johnson, Dave and Rick Broida, *How to Do Everything With MP3 and Digital Music*. New York, NY: McGraw-Hill Osborne Media, 2001.

Kelby, Scott and Kleber Stephenson, *The iTunes for Windows Book: Just What You Need to Unlock the Power of Apple's Digital Jukebox, Music Store, and iPod*. Berkeley, CA: Peachpit Press, 2004.

Leballois, Sandrine, *Le Guide du MP3*. Paris, FRA: Dunod, 2002.

Licklett, Jay, *MP3 FYI: Digital Music Online*. Musk and Lipman Publishing, 2000.

Maes, Jan and Marc Vercammen, *Digital Audio Technology: A Guide to CD, MiniDisc, SACD, DVD(A), MP3 and DAT, 4th Edition*. Boston, MA: Focal Press, 2001.

Mann, Bill, *I Want My MP3: How to Download, Rip and Play Digital Music*. New York, NY: McGraw-Hill Osborne Media, 1999.

McElhearn, Kirk, *iPod Garage*. Upper Saddle River, NJ: Pearson Education, 2004.

Menn, Joseph, *All the Rave: The Rise and Fall of Shawn Fanning's Napster*. New York, NY: Crown Business, 2003.

Merriden, Trevor, *Irresistible Forces: The Business Legacy of Napster and the Growth of the Underground Internet*. Mankato, MN: Capstone Press, 2002.

Notomi, Yasukuni, *iPod Fan Book*. Sebastopol, CA: O'Reilly & Associates, Inc., 2004.

Pohlmann, Ken C., *Principles of Digital Audio, 4th Edition*. New York, NY: McGraw-Hill Professional, 2000.

Rathbone, Andy, *MP3 for Dummies, 2nd Edition*. New York, NY: Hungry Minds, Inc., 2001.

Robertson, Michael and Ron Simpson, *The Official MP3.com Guide to MP3*. MP3.com, 1999.

Sellars, Paul, *(Quick Start) CD Burning*. Bremen,

Germany: Wizoo Publishing, 2001.

Underhill, Rod, *Complete Idiot's Guide to MP3: Music on the Internet*. Farmingdale, NY: Alpha Communications, 2000.

Van Der Wal, Chris, *MP3: From Rip to Record*. Boston, MA: Data Becker, 2001.
Waugh, Ian, *Quick Guide to MP3 and Digital Music*. Norfolk, ENG: PC Publishing, 2001.

White, Ron and Michael White, *MP3 Underground: The Inside Guide to MP3 Music, Napster, RealJukebox, MusicMatch, and Hidden Internet Songs*. Indianapolis, IN: Que, 2000.

Index

P

Z